HIS GUIDING HAND

Alexander S. Fulop

TEACH Services, Inc.
PUBLISHING
www.TEACHServices.com • (800) 367-1844

World rights reserved. This book or any portion thereof may not be copied or reproduced in any form or manner whatever, except as provided by law, without the written permission of the publisher, except by a reviewer who may quote brief passages in a review.

The author assumes full responsibility for the accuracy of all facts and quotations as cited in this book. The opinions expressed in this book are the author's personal views and interpretations, and do not necessarily reflect those of the publisher.

This book is provided with the understanding that the publisher is not engaged in giving spiritual, legal, medical, or other professional advice. If authoritative advice is needed, the reader should seek the counsel of a competent professional.

Copyright © 2014 TEACH Services, Inc.
ISBN-13: 978-1-4796-0412-8 (Paperback)
ISBN-13: 978-1-4796-0413-5 (ePub)
ISBN-13: 978-1-4796-0414-2 (Mobi)
Library of Congress Control Number: 2014955997

All scripture quotations are taken from the New King James Version®. Copyright © 1982 by Thomas Nelson, Inc. Used by permission. All rights reserved.

Published by

www.TEACHServices.com • (800) 367-1844

Table of Contents

Acknowledgements 5
Introduction 7
The Day My Life Changed 10
Venturing Into New Territory 18
Farm Work 24
The Dangerous River 33
Death From the Sky 38
Running for Our Lives 42
Meeting My Savior 48
Fire for My Lord 61
My Sweetheart 67
Separation 73
Entering My New Country 79
The Miraculous Reunion 84
Life Together 92
Relocating to New York 96
Conclusion 106

Acknowledgements

I appreciate the hard work that Kalie Kelch put in to editing my story.

Also, my story would not be possible if it were not for the following physicians who supported me in the medical field and helped me find jobs in my profession:

- Dr. Kassai for hiring me to work for him in his laboratory in Hungary, where I learned the basic anatomy and histology techniques.

- Dr. Mac Gilvery for hiring me as a histology technician and part-time worker at the Worcester City Hospital when I was a student at Atlantic Union College (AUC).

- Dr. H. Rosenkranc for giving me a part-time job at the Worcester Foundation for Experimental Laboratory in Srewsbury, Massachusetts, while I was in college, and for his recommendation to Dr. Mason of Mason Research Institute to be a full-time head technician in his research lab.

- Dr. Reynolds, president of Atlantic Union College, for his care in writing a letter to the president of Hungary requesting the release of my wife and daughter. By his kind action, after five years of waiting, they were allowed to come to America and we were again united as a family.

- Dr. F. Zack for helping me to learn electron microscopy (EM), for his recommendation to work at the New York Medical College in Manhattan, and for his willingness to take me with him to the Methodist Hospital to run the EM laboratory.

- Dr. E. Cramer of SUNY Downstate Medical Center in Brooklyn for allowing me to work for her in electron microscopy research.

I want to thank my loving wife for her patience and faithfulness to me, especially when we were separated while I was in America and she was in Hungary.

And last but not least, I am very grateful to my heavenly Father for His lovingkindness, care, protection, and providence in my life. Without Him I would be nothing, lost in this sinful and complicated world. Praise His holy name for His everlasting goodness toward me and my family.

Introduction

For a long time I debated whether I should write this book and share my life story, a story of joy, sorrows, and trials. One day as I sat in the library of my home in Chattanooga, Tennessee, my mind traveled back to the past history of my life: from childhood when I lived with my parents and siblings in the outskirts of Budapest; when I was small and later years when the tragedy happened with my dad; the separation of my family; the unhappy years living on my grandparents' farm; World War II and the merciless bombings of our cities.

As the stories flooded my mind, I wondered if anyone would be interested in reading about my life, but I felt impressed to share in hopes that my story will touch someone's life and remind them that God is at work in each of our lives through the good and bad times.

I was born into a factory worker's home in the outskirts of the great city of Budapest, called Csepel (pronounced Chapel) at that time. The city was full of hard-working folks who made their meager living serving in Hungary's biggest factory, which was owned by Fred Weisman, a multi-millionaire Jewish businessman. The area most likely resembled the present day lower-income sections of cities such as Chicago, Los Angeles, or New York City. While the parents worked long hours, the kids adapted to city life, which meant aimlessly roaming the streets and looking for mischief. Fights and stealing were quite common.

My parents came from a small village close to the border of Austria in western Hungary. However, my father wanted a better life for his children than working on the farm, so he moved to the city and married a young woman whom his parents felt was of questionable background and did not approve of. Sadly, his parents' concerns about living in the city with its evil vices came to fruition, and my father began to drink, which made life miserable at home.

At age eleven I was taken to my grandparents' farm, which brought with it challenges and hardship. In my teens years World War II descended on us with all its fury. I will never forget the air raids, sirens, bombings, and death. As the Red Army approached, I joined the Hungarian Army; yet I was captured and put in a prison camp.

Amidst all of this I found God and true peace. Of course, this did not mean that life suddenly became easy. Religious persecution and the horrible events of the revolution of 1956 impacted my life. Upon beginning a new life in the United States of America, I was separated from my family for years.

My life has taken twists and turns, but through it all I have seen the hand of providence and care from a loving heavenly Father. I must admit that sometimes His providence was not clear and transparent, and at times I rebelled against God for the things I could not understand. But eventually the storm clouds cleared, and

Introduction

I realized that the sun, like God, had always been there even though it was hidden from my view. It was then that I learned that God not only understood the little details of my life, but He sheltered me with His wings and guided me to the right path.

It is my prayer that my story will give you courage and hope. This life is full of tribulations and trials, but He who gave His life for the sins of the world is interested in every individual on this small planet. My life is a witness to this truth.

So, dear friends, as you read the pages of this book you will see that behind the scenes there is a God who is patiently and lovingly working things out for our good. I have seen the power of God in my life, and I hope you can see His hand in your life too.

Chapter 1

The Day My Life Changed

It all seemed so surreal. My mother, brother, sister, and I arrived at one of the largest cemeteries in Budapest, Hungary, and were greeted with the stark reality that Dad was dead. His body lay in a glass top covered open casket. Our life would never be the same again.

Not too long ago, Dad was a handsome and vibrant man, thinking that he could conquer the world. He was only thirty-five years of age and was an active and talented man, but now he lay still, silent, in the cruel grip of death. Death is an enemy, and I certainly wanted to fight back against it as the thought sunk in that my dad was gone. Death causes many sorrows and those who remain experience a wide range of emotions from sorrow, loneliness, and regret. I wanted to shout, "Death! Get away from here! I still need Dad! I still need his strong hands and his support and guidance in my young life." I was only eleven years old at the time. I felt so lonely and abandoned.

There at the cemetery I stood by his coffin and silently gazed at his lifeless body. His face was pale and his eyes were deeply set within their sockets. His mouth seemed to be frozen in a slightly open position. He appeared much thinner than the last I saw him. Of course, it had been five months ago when he had left home to go to the hospital. Sadly, no one had been with him when he took his last breath.

My young mind was filled with questions. Why did he have to die so young when he had so much to live for? Whose fault was the accident at the factory that led to his death? Although I had questions, the answers remained elusive.

Months before a huge crane lifting a stack of heavy sheet metal had accidentally swung and the stack of sheet metal had hit three workers, one of which was my father. The two other men reported the accident, but my father did not report his injury. Therefore, the two men received compensation for their injury, but my father did not. He thought he was strong and the injuries only superficial. He was a tall, muscular man who was used to heavy labor after growing up on his father's farm. Whatever his condition was, he felt that medical attention was not necessary. He figured that the "little injury" and the superficial wound would heal itself without any interference.

However, about a week after the accident, he began to complain that he was not feeling well. "Something is wrong with me," he said, slightly fearful, to Mom.

"Why don't we call the doctor," my mother suggested.

When the doctor arrived, he asked my father some questions. Then, after examining him, he looked up from his stethoscope straight into my father's eyes and said, "Mr. Fulop (pronounced Philip), I do not know exactly what is wrong, but your liver seems to be rather enlarged. I suggest that you go to the hospital for a more complete examination."

The next day he went to the hospital. He expected to be in and out the same day or at most a few days. However, after a thorough examination, they discovered that my father's liver had been damaged by the impact of the metal hitting his abdomen. From that point on his health rapidly deteriorated. Soon, he was not able to eat, causing him to lose weight. His bad habits of smoking and drinking had weakened his liver, and it did not have the resilience it needed to repair itself from the traumatic injury. He remained hospitalized for weeks with my mom visiting him regularly. She wanted to take us to visit, but he did not want us to see him in his declining and weakened condition.

One day he was waiting for my mom at the door. "Eszter (pronounced Ayster), I am sorry, but I have some more bad news to tell you," he said in a choked up voice. "A further examination has discovered that besides my injured liver, my lungs have become infected with tuberculosis (TB)."

My mom almost fainted. She was struggling to cope with the shock of his injured liver and the fact that he might not get better. This latest bit of news was just as terrifying as the last.

"Are they sure, Sandor (pronounced Shondor)?" she asked after recovering from the shocking news.

My father replied, "Yes, the X-ray shows that it is very serious. I need immediate medical treatment because of its severity. They have recommended that I go to a TB sanatorium."

My mother sat there listening; her head spun as the tragic news unfolded. She knew well what that meant. At that time in Hungary, there was a TB epidemic. Anyone whose condition was rather run down was unable to tolerate the onslaught of that dreadful infectious disease. She knew deep down that this meant his days were numbered. There was no cure for TB in the late 1930s. One of my

The Day My Life Changed

sister Sari's (pronounced Shory) friends, a girl of just fourteen, had recently died of TB. A few months later Mary's sister followed her to the grave from the same disease.

Not only was it frightening to think that Dad had TB, but Mom was also fearful that the disease might infect other members of our family. We, too, were also very worried about what might happen to us if we contracted TB—that possibility frightened us all.

Within a few days, Dad was admitted to a tuberculosis center not far from Budapest. The facility was situated on a mountainside where the air was fresh and clean. They gave him the best treatments they had in an effort to save his life, but nothing helped. His health deteriorated rapidly. It was a trying time for all of us. It was a soul-searching time, especially for Dad. He was broken-hearted at the thought that his fourteen years of marriage to my mother were coming to an end.

He recognized that he had done many terrible things to his family because of his drinking habit, especially in the last two years. Now he had time to think about those incidents and feel sorry for what he had done. He well remembered the times he had spent his week's salary on alcohol, only to come home in a drunken stupor. His drinking habit meant less time for his family and the necessities of life such at rent and food. Even though he earned good wages, most of his money was spent on alcohol.

To make matters worse, when he was drunk, he became mean and cruel. Many times he attempted to hit us for seemingly no reason at all. My mom stood between us and took the brunt of his anger. One time he came home drunk and sat down to eat some ham and bread. I was sitting next to him at the table, as were my two uncles, Istvan and Mihaly (pronounced Ishtvon and Mehaay). Mom was very sick and in bed, but she scold him. Dad was clearly embarrassed at being reprimanded in front of my uncles, and in anger he slashed the end of the wooden bed frame where my mother lay with the knife he was using to eat with.

We children ran for safety. At that, my two uncles, fearing that the next slash of the knife might be directed at Mom, wrestled the knife from his grip and pushed him out the door. He fell from our three-foot high terrace to the ground, got up, and wandered away.

Uncle Istvan insisted that we spend the night at his home for he did not trust that my dad would come home sober and calm. Two days later Dad showed up at my uncle's home walking with the aid of a crutch. He had broken his leg when falling from the terrace. He looked so sad and pitiful that my heart broke for him.

"Eszter, I am so sorry for what I did," Dad confessed, knowing that he had upset and frightened her so badly. "Please come back home. I swear that I will never do anything like that again."

Mom felt compassion toward him and told him she would come home with him. "OK, Sandor. We forgive you and will all go home together."

Although he was fine for the next few weeks, he did not give up his drinking, and within a short period of time he fell back into his old habits.

Now, in his suffering and loneliness at the sanatorium, he contemplated all of the mistakes he had made. He recalled the days he had been mean and cruel to us, and he deeply regretted his actions and choices.

One day when mom visited him, he apologized and asked her for forgiveness. "Eszter, I am so very sorry for my cruelty toward you and the hard times I've given you. I should never have started drinking. I am so sorry for the pain and suffering I put you and the children through."

"It's alright, Sandor. Let's not talk about that now. I forgive you. Let's just forget about it." She still loved my father and was willing to put all that behind her. "The important thing now is that you regain your health and come back home where you belong."

But her wish did not come true. Neither the treatments, nor the fresh mountain air improved his condition, and within five months of being admitted to the hospital, the damaged liver and TB claimed his life.

Our little family was devastated. This was the first time I had experienced death, and the heart-wrenching feeling I had at his funeral was almost more than I could bear. As we stood there together looking at the casket, my nine-year-old brother, Lajos (pronounced Loyosh), suddenly said, "Daddy is sleeping. I will go wake him up!"

He loosened his grip on my mother's hand and lunged forward toward the lifeless body. Mom reached out, pulling him back saying, "No, my son, he is not sleeping.... He ... is ... dead." Then she broke down in agonizing sobs as she realized that her husband and the father of their children was forever gone from this earth.

Later in my life when I accepted Christ and began studying His Word I found that my brother spoke truth when he said that our father was sleeping, for Jesus told His disciples that death is like sleep, for the dead know nothing. My brother innocently thought he would be able to "wake him up," but the only person who can wake the dead is the Son of God. During His ministry on earth, Jesus raised dead people to life, and He will do so again at the second coming (1 Thess. 4:15-18; notice that he also calls "sleeping" of the dead).

Oh how I wish I could have known about the state of the dead at that time when I stood by my father's casket. How much easier it would have been for all of us to bear the inconsolable sorrow that we experienced at the funeral. How lighter the grief would have been for Mom. How easier we could have faced the trying events to come in the days ahead. If only we had the knowledge and hope of the resurrection.

As we stood there, four men came and closed my father's casket and carried it to a two-horse carriage that bore him to the graveyard. We followed the procession on foot. Unfortunately, no other relatives were there at his funeral. It took about fifteen minutes to travel to the graveyard; however, it seemed like an hour's walk. It was the saddest, loneliest, and gloomiest walk I can remember. It was a foggy, rainy day—it seemed as if nature was even weeping with us. The darkness seemed to enshroud my soul.

We were Lutherans at the time, so our minister conducted the gravesite service. I don't remember any of the words he said, but he was a godly man, so I'm sure his word were kind and assuring.

I had studied with him after school for a few months. My brother and I would go to his parish where he gave us lessons on faith, told us about the Bible and God, and instructed us on the life of the great Christian reformer Martin Luther. He taught us that Luther stood fast in his conviction that man is saved by grace, and not by works (Rom. 1:17; Gal. 2:16). Of course, James tells us that faith bears the fruit of good works (James 2:14, 17). I am ever grateful to that Lutheran minister for the strong faith he encouraged me to have in the Bible, which later helped me to study the precious Word of God and extend my knowledge of Him and about all biblical doctrines.

Of course, in my moment of grief at the gravesite, I forgot all of those spiritual studies and the wonderful words that we heard about God and His love for us. I couldn't even listen to the minister. All I could do was cry with the rest of my family. Cry for the loss of a life. Cry for what could have been.

Now that my dad was gone I tried to think of all the good memories I had of him. I wanted to forget the bad memories, the time when he came home drunk and scared us with his violent temper. I wanted to remember the early days when dad would come home from work in the afternoon to my mom's delicious cooking and we would all eat together at the table. After the meal, Dad would take out one of his musical instruments and play for us. We often joined in with our voices, singing along with whatever tune he was playing.

On weekends, we often had guests in our home. After a big, delicious dinner, we would play games and sang old Hungarian country songs. Or we would watch him work on his beautiful oil paintings. Many times I wondered how he became so talented seeing that he had only completed six grades of schooling in his small hometown.

Our life had been filled with excitement and joy until he began drinking, and those were the memories I wanted to hold on to. However, it was hard, because the most recent memories were of sadness, loss, and fear.

At the end of the funeral service, the four men lowered the casket into the grave and began to shovel dirt on top of the coffin. The scraping, drumming, and rasping sounds that came from the hole after each shovel of dirt caused my mother to break down. She wept, her loud sobs piercing the air. We held her tightly and tried to comfort her, but our tears joined hers as we stood huddled together in the graveyard. I thought that our crying would never end.

Chapter 2

Venturing Into New Territory

After the burial we somehow managed to get home by enduring an hour-long ride on a streetcars. A few days later my mom gathered us together to tell us something important. She looked so serious that I knew whatever she had to say would affect my life, which it indeed did!

"My dear children," she begun, "I know that your dad's death has affected you. Regardless of how many bad experiences we had in the past, we all forgave him and miss him very much." She continued. "Your father's illness and death have greatly impacted my health. As you know, I have pleurisy. During your father's illness, I tried my best to hold on. Many times I dragged my sick body to see him, which led me to exhaustion. The doctor has told me that if I want to survive and not follow him to the grave I need to rest and regain my strength. That means that I cannot work for a time. Therefore, there will not be any income coming into our house. Unfortunately, this means that I cannot take care of you."

I knew this decision wasn't easy for her. She said, "I

made arrangements for you boys to stay in our hometown. Sanyi (pronounced Shoney, which is a nickname for Sandor), you will go to your grandparent's place in Ostffyasszonyfa and help them on the farm. Lali (pronounced Loly), you will go to the same town, but you will be helping on a different farm."

After taking a deep breath, she continued, "Sari (pronounced Shory), you will stay with me. I will need you to get a job so that you can support the two of us until I am well." Sari was only thirteen years old at the time.

The next day Mom gathered the few things we boys had, and we boarded the train headed for our destination, which was 160 kilometers west of Budapest, close to the Austrian border. The trip took about six hours, but we didn't mind for there was so much to see and talk about. We were very fascinated in the people getting on and off the train. There were well dressed and poorly dressed people with small luggage and big cases. Some ladies carried eggs or fruits in big baskets to sell at the market in the nearby cities and towns. I carefully watched them because everything was completely new to me.

We also saw beautiful lands and forests. Some areas featured green grass with cows and horses grazing on the hills. Other areas boasted of wheat and cornfields. I wondered, *Is this the kind of land I going to live in? What kind life is waiting for me? What will I do on the farm?* These and many other questions flew through my mind in quick succession.

Although there was a certain level of excitement at the prospect of living on the farm, the thought of being separated from my mom made me shiver. Father was gone; my sister was with my mom; and my brother was assigned to work somewhere else. I wondered when we would all be together again. I also wondered in my grandparents would like me.

I did not know much about my extended family on either side, but what I had heard recently about my dad's parents made me very uncomfortable. Somehow I found out that they opposed the marriage of my dad to mom because of a girl named Anna. Later I discovered, to my great surprise, that Anna was my half-sister who had been borne out of wedlock. I had seen her at my other grandparent's house when we were on vacation, but I had thought she was my mom's youngest sister, which wasn't too hard to picture since she had fourteen brothers and sisters. I just assumed that she was my youngest aunt, being only six years older than I was.

My mom was embarrassed about the mistake of her youth and had chosen to keep quiet about the situation; however, one day an older cousin of mine "spilled the beans."

"Did you know that Anna is your sister?"

"What are you talking about?" I asked him.

"You clearly don't know. Anna is your half-sister."

When I questioned my mom about it, she told me the full story. She had fallen in love with a young man named Ferenci (pronounced Farancy). Unfortunately, one day she turned up pregnant, but because they loved each other and wanted to be married, my mom thought a quick marriage would be the best to "cover up" their mistake and save her the embarrassment of a pregnancy out of wedlock.

Ferenci went to my mom's parents and asked for her hand in marriage. "Mr. and Mrs. Varga, I am very sorry that Eszter is pregnant. I love her and would like to marry her. Would you let me marry Eszter?"

His intention was genuine and honest. He was financially stable, but he was Catholic, which was a big problem for my grandparents. As Lutherans, they could not imagine their daughter marrying a Catholic. Such a "mixed" marriage was unthinkable in their little town in which everyone fell one or the other denomination. And because my grandparents were "faithful Lutherans," the answer was "NO!" Regardless of how the "lovers" wanted to marry and save their reputations, they were not permitted a "mixed" relationship. My grandma said, "Even if I have to raise the child myself, I won't let a 'papist' come into our family."

My mom gave birth to a beautiful girl whom she loved a lot, but she was unhappy about her parent's decision. She decided to leave home as soon as she could. And her "opportunity" soon arrived.

Ferenci supported his newborn daughter by giving things to my grandma. Ferenci married shortly after my grandparents' rejection of his marriage proposal and soon had other children with his wife. Because they lived next door to my grandma's house, Anna soon wanted to play with the neighbor's children, of which she did not know were her half-brothers and half-sisters. But Fenenci's wife, knowing who she was, and not wanting to be reminded of her husband's past, treated her harshly. "Go home! You cannot play here!" she told her.

Anna ran home crying and told her grandparents the event in tears. Grandpa walked across the street and told her, "Don't treat Anna like that! She does not have anything to do with how she came into this world!"

When my father and mother got together, Grandma and Grandpa Fulop did not approve since they knew about her past. However, Father loved her and was determined to marry her. But how could they do it? Religion was not a problem because they were both Lutherans. On the other hand, if they married without the permission of his parents, they would be judged harshly in the small village. So they decided to run away from home and get married in Budapest. My father never saw his parent after that.

Knowing pieces of my parents' story, I had mixed feelings about meeting my grandparents. Will they accept the child of a disobedient son? I wondered. Will they forgive their runaway son and welcome his offspring into their home?

Before I was ready, the conductor's announcement brought me back to reality. "We are arriving in Ostffyasszonyfa within a few minutes." Mom, my brother, and I gathered our things and waited until the train came to a complete stop before disembarking.

It was late afternoon when we arrived at the railroad station. To my surprise, Ferenci, Anna's father, was waiting for us with his taxi. He had become one of the richest businessmen in the town. Besides owning farm equipment, he owned a taxi too. I could not read my mom's mind, but her face displayed a mix of emotions at seeing her old boyfriend and the father of her first child.

Mom decided that she would drop me off first because my grandparent's house was on the way to town. As we neared our destination, I spotted Grandma coming out of the house. When she saw us get out of the car, she came to the gate. "I see you arrived safely," she said with reservation, yet her tone was kind. "Please, come in," she said and opened the gate for us. I don't remember her hugging us or not, but she was friendly. She gave us some food to eat. And then Mom told her all that had happened in the last six months. She listened quietly, but I could detect on her face a great sorrow at losing her son so early in his life. I did not see any tears in Grandma's eyes, but I assumed that she had already shed them.

All to soon mom left with my brother to deliver him to another farmer's house, leaving me with Grandma.

I unpacked my things and sat down on a wooden chair. I felt a tremendous emptiness in my heart. I wanted to run after my mom, but I knew that wasn't possible.

At sunset the rest of the family—Grandpa, Uncle Jozsef, Aunt Roza, and Kalman—arrived from the field and greeted me kindly. Grandma gave them supper, and before long I was told to get ready for bed.

"Sanyi, your bed is ready for you in the stable," my uncle said.

"In the stable?" I asked. "I've never slept in a stable. I've always had a nice bed to sleep on in the bedroom!"

"We don't have enough space in the bedroom for another bed," he simply stated.

"Don't worry, Sanyi," interrupted Kalman, "I put plenty of straw at the corner and fenced it with boards, and I put a big blanket over it. There is also a big coat to cover yourself with. I also sleep in the stable. It is not as bad as you think. The cows are very friendly and quiet creatures," he concluded.

My new sleeping arrangement was strange to me, yet it was my new life. I found my designated corner in the stable and lay down on the blanket. It was soft and comfortable. As the light faded I listened to the cows. Because I was so tired from the activities of the day, I slowly drifted off into a deep sleep.

Chapter 3

Farm Work

At about seven o'clock the next morning I woke up to the sound of early morning farm chores. The stable doors were open wide. Grandpa, Uncle Jozsef, and Kalman were already busy cleaning up the barn. They were bringing in clean straw for the animals and brushing them with an iron brush to get the dirt off. Suddenly Grandma appeared with a big bucket to milk the cows. She pulled a three-legged stool under her, sat down near the cow, and held the bucket between her knees. Then she squeezed the cow's udders and the milk shot into the bucket.

When the work was done in the barn, we assembled in the kitchen for breakfast. We drank the fresh milk and enjoyed hearty, homemade bread from Grandma's brick oven.

After breakfast Uncle Jozsef told me what my chores would be, which included watching the cows. He was a very humble and friendly man, just like the biblical Joseph. He never used any bad words; he was kind and friendly to everyone, yet he was also very strict. In fact, one time I miscalculated the time it would take me to get home, and I arrived too early with the cows. I was supposed to leave the field in enough time to get home just before sunset. But when I arrived home, the sun was still high in the sky. My uncle felt that I must be "corrected," so he made me kneel on a rough cement block for hours.

Another time I was watching the cows between two fields of corn. It was a very hot summer day, so I decided to cool off in a nearby creek. To avoid the possibility of the cows ruining the cornfields while I swam, I led them to the creek so that I could keep an eye on them. I was enjoying myself in the cool water when I looked up and saw my uncle standing there with a whip in his hand.

"What are you doing?" he shouted. Then he grabbed my hand and gave me a good whipping. I was very upset and felt that he was the meanest man in the world. In my desperation to retaliate, I told my uncle that he was not my father and shouldn't punish me so hard. But many years later I thanked him for helping me to become a responsible and decent man. He never had his own children because he married a widow in his late fifties who had four children of her own. Sadly, she had a temper and would lash out at him and hit him. I often wondered how such a humble and kind person could marry a mean woman.

On that first morning my uncle took me to the barn and gave me instructions on how to care for the cows and what grasslands to feed them in. After he was done speaking, he turned the cows loose, and as soon as they passed the gate, they turned in the right direction. They knew every corner of the village, where to turn right or left and where the grassland was. I was amazed. My uncle and I simply followed them as they walked.

When we got to the field, my uncle outlined the territory where I was supposed to keep the cows. Two sides were lined with acacia trees, one side was a road, and the other side was a wheat field. He told me to constantly be on guard.

In Hungary they do not build fences to keep in the animals. If a farmer has a large herd of cattle, he hires a man to watch over them. If he has only a few, like my folks had only six to ten, a boy or teenager was assigned the task.

As soon as my uncle finished informing me of my job responsibilities, he turned to me and said, "Sanyi, you understand your duties. Now I am going home. Keep them in the right place," he continued. "Remember, they are very smart creatures. If you do not watch them constantly, they will move beyond the territory and damage the nearby farms."

Growing up in the city, it felt strange to be alone with these creatures in an open field. I was used to city life—people, streetcars, noise, and activities. Everything was so quiet in the country, and there was no one around for me to talk to. I felt so lonely that I began to cry. After crying for a bit, I tried to occupy my mind with something to forget my loneliness. I looked around and discovered that behind the narrow acacia forest was a potato field. A few days later I became distracted with my toys while working in the field and discovered that my "charges" were happily eating the delicious potato plant leaves. I quickly chased them back to our land, but the damage was done. They had eaten a ten-by-ten foot area of potato plants down to the ground.

I was afraid to tell anyone about what had happened, but a few days later the owner discovered the damage. He estimated the loss, and my grandparents gave him a big sack of potatoes to cover the damage. They did not physically punish me, but they severely scolded me and warned of greater consequences if it happened again.

Day after day I took the cows to the field and watched them. I soon learned that on the other side of the road, the Catholic Church owned a larger piece of property. They hired a young man from Yugoslavia to take care of their fifty to seventy cows. Apparently the boys from Yugoslavia were cheaper to hire than those of us who were locals. I wondered why the priests needed hundreds of acres of lands and so many beasts when they were supposed to minister to the soul of their parishioners. I tried to be friendly with one of the Yugoslavian boys, but he was mean and quick to flash his pocketknife in warning to stay away from him.

On the priest's land, as we used to call it, were a lot of prairie dogs, which are somewhat smaller than their American counterpart. The farmers hated them because they damaged their wheat fields. By one farmer's estimation, one family of prairie dogs, which could be as little as eight of them, could hoard about sixty-to-eighty kilos of wheat for a winter season in their burrows. I estimated that there were about fifty prairie dog families in the priest's fifty acres, which meant that thousands of kilos of wheat were being destroyed each season.

Because I had so much time on my hands to think, I decided to "help" the farmers eliminate the prairie dogs while having some fun at the same time. I used my pocketknife to fabricate a little horse wagon with wheels. I just needed a "horse" to pull it, so I decided to catch a prairie dog. I made a hook and placed it over the entrance of one of their holes. When one came out of the hole, I tightened the loop around its neck. Then I pulled it out of the hole by the neck. Next, I hooked it to my wagon while holding onto the leash of the animal, and as the poor creature ran away from me, it pulled my wagon. Unfortunately, my least favorite part of this game was that when I finished playing I had to dispose of the prairie dog.

I watched the cows seven days a week without any break. Sometimes I was so discouraged that I cried all day. On Sunday my grandparents and uncle stopped their routine work, but the cows had to eat, so I had to be with them even on Sundays. The only difference was that my family brought me cooked food instead of sending me with a sack lunch consisting of fruit and bread.

Each morning before I left for the field my grandma gave me a bag of food for the day. But because I had good appetite, I hardly left any for the afternoon hours. This meant that I was hungry way before it was time to come home for the evening. Once in a while I got extra food from the river guide's nearby garden. The people were very friendly and were willing to share their fruits and vegetables with me. After enjoying their friendship for a year, the family left and a new river guide moved into the house.

One day a younger boy and I decided to help ourselves to some fruit from the orchard. We entered through a hole in the fence and began eating the delicious produce when suddenly we heard somebody say, "Hey, boys, what are you doing in my orchard?"

We turned around to find the river guide standing near the hole in the fence. "Come out immediately!" he commanded. We were surprised and shocked. What now? We looked at each other, unsure of what to do next. We could not escape. I told my younger friend to go first. As soon as he stepped through the hole, the river guide grabbed him. I then quickly jumped through the hole and took off running. Because he really wanted to catch me, since I was the older one, he released my friend and lunged for me. But I was faster. Now my friend was free as well, and we both ran like the wind.

In the evening we all assembled in the house to each our "big meal" together. As a growing boy, I had a tremendous appetite. Most of the times, I wanted to eat more than my grandma allowed, for she would say, "You can't eat more than your uncle."

I soon discovered that my favorite season was winter because, although it was very cold, I could go to school with other children instead of watching the cows by myself. School ran from December to March because of the farming season. With the school year being so short, the teacher tried to teach us as much as possible in as little time as possible. We went to school from 8:00 a.m. to 5:00 p.m. with a break at noon for lunch. Besides the regular subjects, the teachers taught me about the Bible and Jesus' redeeming grace. I loved every bit of my day at the Lutheran school. It was the beginning of my religious experience and my love of the Bible.

I also loved Sundays because I got to go to church with Grandma and Aunt Roza. They were the only two members of my family who regularly went to church. Although the rest of the family were "good" people, they never cared for religious services. I occasionally saw Uncle Jozsef at church, but Grandpa never went.

The church used an old-fashioned pump organ that you had to pedal in order to produce any sound. Every Sunday some of us young people were given the job of pumping the organ with our feet. If we did not pedal properly or we slowed down, the organ sounded funny. At times we slowed down on purpose to hear the funny sounds coming from the organ, but the organist would quickly look at us with scolding eyes, and we would resume our duties.

During the winter if we were not in school, we were chopping wood with Grandpa. I remember one time I almost cut off his finger. He held a piece of uneven wood on a big flat log. It was my job to split it with a huge axe.

I swung the axe high in the air and aimed for the wood, but because of my inexperience and the weight of the axe, I missed the log and hit his finger. Fortunately, I did not cut his finger off, but I did injure his hand. He cursed at me and said he was going to beat me, but I ran away from him. Within a few minutes he calmed down and said, "Sanyi, come back. Let's continue splitting the wood."

Most Sunday afternoons I had a few hours to go to my friend's house to play. Those days the toys were simple and inexpensive, and many times we made them ourselves. We also made up a variety of games to pass the time. One game was played with clay balls. The goal was to see who could throw the balls and get them to land closest to the wall from a distance of fifteen feet away. The winner got to keep the balls for that round. One time I remember coming home with a big bag of balls that I had won. My grandparents felt sorry for the losers and told me to return the balls.

The longer I stayed with my grandparents the more I realize that Grandma was the one running the household. It wasn't that she was a domineering or headstrong woman. It was just that she had a good head on her shoulders and seemed to know what to do. She was an excellent cook and baker, and she was very smart. She was also a God-fearing woman who read her Bible regularly, especially the Psalms. Many times I noticed her praying with an open Bible. I slowly found out about some of the hardships she had experienced and the reason she was so knowledgeable about the farm.

In 1913 Grandpa decided to find his fortune in Canada, so he left Grandma and the children in Hungary and headed across the ocean. Arriving in Canada, he worked in a coal mine and saved his earning to take back home. He planned to only stay one year, but right when he was scheduled to return World War I broke out, and he was detained for four years until the war ended. In the meantime, Grandma survived with the children on her own. She even dealt with the horror of losing their house and everything they owned to a fire.

When Grandpa returned home, they bought a house and a few acres of land and some cattle with the money he had saved while working in Canada. Life was somewhat easier on the little farm.

I marveled at how Grandma could keep track of when everything needed to be done. She knew what land needed to be plowed or sowed and when. As "commander in chief" of the farm, she often gave us instructions by asking questions, such as, "Jozsef, did you check the wheat field? Is it ready for the harvest?" Everyone gave Grandma a report of their activities, and then she would give the order of what to do next.

I settled into life on the farm with my grandparents and uncle, but I had questions about the young man who lived with us. His name was Kalman, and he was seventeen years old, four years older than I was. However, no one wanted to talk about where he came from. Even Grandma was quiet when I asked about him.

It wasn't until years later when I was visiting some relatives in the town that I discovered he was my cousin, son of my oldest aunt, Lidi. But because no one knew who the father was, they kept it a secret that he was a part of the family. Aunt Lidi had died when he was a toddler, but with no father on his birth certificate, no one knew his origin, so they kept it quiet. Sadly, just as Kalman mysteriously came into this world, he mysteriously disappeared from this world while fighting in World War II. No one knows the date or location of his death. The last communication we had was that he was being sent to the front lines of the Hungarian Army in their defense against the Russians. Most likely he was killed in a battle and buried with the 300,000 or so other Hungarian solders somewhere in the snowy mountains of Russia.

When I found out about his death, I felt an ache in my heart, for I now knew that he was my cousin. I have fond memories of our time together on the farm. I hope that I will see him among the saints when Jesus returns.

Chapter 4

The Dangerous River

I settled into life on the farm and accepted my job of watching the cows. One day not long after my arrival, a letter arrived from my mother addressed to my grandparents. My mother had had a dream that I was in great danger. The only danger my grandma could think of was the river near the grassland where I took the cows, so they told me not to go into it because many people had been drown in the river. Taking their advice, I decided not to go into the water, even if I had a tremendous urge to cool myself off. Unfortunately, my resolve was tested one day by another cattle boy.

One day while I was sitting by the riverbank I heard somebody calling my name. "Sanyi, Sanyi!" I looked in the direction of the voice, and I saw the cattle boy from the land adjacent to ours. "Come over and help me get my cows into the river!" he shouted. Many ranchers would drive their cattle into the water to clean them.

"No, I can't!" I responded.

"Why not?" he asked.

"Because my folks told me not to go into the water. It is too dangerous."

"O, come on!" he argued. "They will never know that you were in the water."

My friend's invitation was very tempting. Yet I had another objection. "But I cannot swim."

"No problem," he said. "You can hold the tail of a cow. She will take you in and out of the water without difficulty."

It sounded safe, and since I had a great desire to cool off, I went along with the idea. Before we were knee high in the water, I already held the tail of a cow. As we walked along, the water got deeper. A few more steps and it was chest deep, and suddenly we were floating. *Not bad!* I thought. *Hooray! I am swimming with the cow.* I was holding firmly of its tail. But my joy was short-lived. My friend swam over to me, and deciding that I needed to get my head wet, he pushed the back of the cow down into the water so that I would go under the water with the cow. If I had held onto the tail, everything probably would have been all right, but I panicked and thought I was drowning when my head went under the water. As my fear consumed me, I let go of the cow's tail. As soon as I did, I sank deeper into the water. No mater how hard I tried to get up to the surface, I seemed to sink deeper and deeper. As I struggled for my life, four thoughts went through my mind in lightening speed: 1) This is it—my life is coming to an end; 2) I will die because I disobeyed my folks; 3) I will never see my loved ones again; and 4) I remember Mom and Dad teaching me about a God in heaven who hears our prayers; maybe He can save me.

In helpless desperation I cried out, "My God!" I could not say anything else, for my strength was gone and I was drowning. Then a miracle happened of which I never forget. Suddenly I felt as if I was being lifted to the surface of the water. As my head came out of the water, I gulped air into my lungs. God had saved me from certain death.

After his immature trick, my friend realized that I had let go of the tail and had not come back up out of the water. He panicked. He swam around the area where I had disappeared from his view, but he couldn't see me. Providentially, when I came up to the surface, he was right there and took me to the shore. I was so exhausted that I lay on the shore for a long time.

There was another miracle also. My cows stayed in the same place the whole time I was in the water. They were grazing quietly, like I had been with them the whole time.

When I reached town with the cows that evening, one of the ladies standing at her gate said to me, "I heard you almost drowned, and somebody had to save you!"

I figured that if she knew the story my folks also had heard about it. Sure enough, they did! Their first words were, "We have heard that somebody had to rescue you from the water! We told you not to go into the river. You did not listen to us!"

Their words were true, yet they were like hammers to my already troubled body, mind, and soul. They gave me feel so bad that I almost felt like I was drowning again. Yet another feeling washed over me that said, "Cheer up, young man! You are alive; you have been saved!" What a delightful thought! God had heard my prayer, and I was alive! This comforted me and gave me inner peace.

As I listened to them scold me, I had a strange thought, No one is talking about the boy who convinced me to swim and who played a trick on me. Instead of talking about the negative part he played in this event, they see him as a hero! No one really wants to hear the full story.

I learned a lesson that day that obedience is a good thing. It will save you from lots of troubles. Yet, if we make a poor decision and we are in trouble, God is still with us and hears our desperate cries for help.

Later on when I had more Bible knowledge, I discovered the great truth of those four thoughts that came to my mind in that great struggle. We all feel uncomfortable talking about death. It is like an unwanted enemy in our life. Actually, it really is the enemy of mankind. We have a fear of death. Of course, someone who believes in God does not need to fear the enemy, for they have a Savior and their future is sure. Therefore, our fear of death dissipates. I have seen many precious saints peacefully go to sleep, trusting in His everlasting love and the promise of the resurrection at His second coming. The good news is that regardless of our shortcomings and sins, if we confess them and ask God to help us He is willing to forgive us and He is willing to help us out of our troubles. Thinking back to my story, I was lost in the water and condemned to die because of my disobedience to my folks. But by His grace I was saved. What a great biblical truth that is! The Bible says that the wages of sin is death, but thank God the gift of His Son gives us eternal life. If we believe in Him, He will rescue us from "drowning," and He will give us eternal life. Praise His holy name!

The shock and strain of drowning affected my heart, and I noticed that I had an irregular heartbeat. The doctor said that I should grow out of it. He gave me some medication, and a few weeks later my heartbeat went back to normal. Praise God that my heart is still beating! A few weeks later, I went beck to my usual work.

Time moved forward, and before I knew it, two years slipped by. Two years of loneliness and separation from my mother and brother and sister. I longed to be with them again. I was so lonely working in the field watching the cows. I had no one to talk to; my heart ached for companionship. I cried almost every day.

I was thirteen years old now, but I was bearing the weight of the world on my young shoulders. I missed my family and longed to be with them. I longed to feel my mother's embrace and eat her delicious meals. I longed to spend time with my siblings and laugh and play together. I understood that my mother had more chances to treat her illness in the city instead of in this small town, but it didn't help the ache in my heart.

I cried for all that I had lost and all that I longed for. Then suddenly, a miracle happened!

As the tears were flowing, I saw a figure approaching me. I couldn't tell who it was because the tears were blurring my vision. I quickly wiped at my eyes so that I could see better. A woman was approaching, and the closer she got, the more she looked like my mother! When she was close enough for me to clearly see, I ran to her.

"Mom, how did you get here?" I cried as we embraced.

"My dear son, I had the feeling that you are not well," she said, pushing me away from her so that she could see my face. "I had an urge to come visit."

"Oh, Mom, I have missed you so much! It is breaking my heart to be apart! I miss Lajos and Sari, too. I wish we could all be back together again."

"Yes, my son, I miss you too!" she said. "It is evident that you are not happy here. No mater how hard our life may be, I will take you with me. Let's go get your brother and go home to Budapest. I, too, want us to be a family again!"

Within few days she had gathered all of our things and the three of us headed to Budapest.

Chapter 5

Death From the Sky

When we arrived back in Budapest, I learned that my sister was working in the same factory that my dad had been an employee at and where he had sustained his injuries that latter led to his death. The factory made everything under the sun, from kitchen tools to machinery, such as tractors, motorcycles, and bicycles, just to name a few. My sister worked as a secretary.

Soon after arriving in the city, she helped me get a job as a messenger for the *Utokalkulacio* office, which means "calculation after the events." In other words, this office was responsible for evaluating the items they sold to determine if it was profitable or worthless. My job was to carry information from one place to another, traveling from the main factory to an office in Budapest. It took me more than half an hour by streetcar to deliver an item, but I loved my job because I liked to travel. After delivering the mail, I would help the seven office workers sort papers or run errands. They loved me and seemed to have a special interest in me because I had lost my father.

Death From the Sky

During this time Hungary was deeply involved in the war. The year was 1943-1944, and the Americans had begun sending planes into Europe. They began bombing their targets, which included locations in Hungary.

The first attack I remember occurred when I was headed to Budapest. I was very close to my destination when the sirens began to sound. Our streetcar immediately stopped, and everybody on board quickly got off and ran to a bomb shelter. I ran into a nearby building and headed for the basement, of which they had designated as a "bomb shelter." Because the building was located in the very center of a big square, all kinds of people were finding refuge in the basement—rich, poor, well dressed, poorly dressed, streetcar conductors, street cleaners. Everyone was on equal footing, for all had the same desire to survive.

Soon the sound of planes humming overhead could be heard. We could also hear the artillery units on the nearby mountainside shooting at them. Everybody was scared to death. Than the planes began to unload their bombs. We heard a whistling sound and a tremendous explosion not far from us. I knew that an oil refinery was close by, and I figured that that was their target.

Hearing the horrible sounds outside, many people began to cry. Some prayed silently, others prayed out loud. I will never forget the prayer of one well-dressed woman who was decked out with jewelry. She cried a loud with a trembling voice, "My God, have mercy on me! If You help me now, I will be more generous to the poor!"

I was curious as to what was happening outside, so I crept toward the door and peeked out. The metal casing from the artillery were all over the street and were still falling from the sky as they continued their attack on the planes. Not thinking about my own safety, I was worried about my sister and decided to go find her. I ran out to the street, but a police officer saw me and yelled, "Get back in the shelter!"

I quickly hit near a big gate, and when he was not looking, I continued on my quest to find my sister. I ran from doorway to doorway when the police were not around. I looked back toward the oil refinery and saw black smoke billowing into the sky. The planes had hit their target.

After running for about twenty minutes, I reached my destination and found that my sister and many others were still in the bomb shelter. Everybody surrounded me and asked me what was going on out there. I was glad that they were all right. I told them what I had seen as I traveled from near the main office back to their location. Most of all, they were glad I was safe.

When the air raid ceased, the office manager let everybody go home. When we emerged from the basement and went into the street, we saw heavy smoke filling the sky in the direction of the oil refinery. It was still burning in full capacity. The streetcars were not running because the tracks had been damaged in the bombing. As we walked, we saw firsthand the damage that had occurred. When we rounded one corner, we found that a whole block of apartment buildings had been leveled. People were looking for their family members among the rubble. We met a man who was looking for his wife. "This was our apartment building," he said, pointing to the pile of concrete. "Our home is gone, and I don't know where my wife is."

I hoped against hope that he would find his wife, but I knew that many had been killed when the building collapsed. As we continued to walk, we saw other houses in ruins and more people looking for their loved ones.

After about two hours of walking, we reached our home. Luckily, our area of town had not been damaged.

The following night the planes came back again. We lived close to the factory, which appeared to be their primary target that evening. Unfortunately, some of the planes missed their targets again and dropped them in the populated areas of the city. We hid in the bomb shelter that had been dug in our backyard and waited for the sirens to cease their wailing. After the attack, we went back to bed, knowing that the morning would bring sadness and sorrow as we examined the damages in our neighborhood. The next day we were greeted by a pitiful scenery. Houses lay in ruins while people searched for their relatives.

From that time on, almost every day and night the planes bombed our area. It was a nerve-wrecking experience. It was too hard to bear, so we decided to leave Budapest and go to my grandparents' farm.

I was now sixteen years old, and although it was safer on the farm and we didn't have to worry about nightly bombings, our country was still not doing well in the war. The Russians were rapidly approaching, breaking through every defense. With this news, I decided to run away to the west with my brother and a few young men from the town.

Chapter 6

Running for Our Lives

Shortly after our departure from my grandparents' town, we encountered a small Hungarian Army unit made up of mostly officers. For our safety and protection, we volunteered to join them. After their private evaluation of our request, they accepted us with one condition: we would be responsible for caring for the "livestock" that they had for food. We agreed to the arrangement. When they stopped, we watched the livestock as they grazed beside the road. The men gave me a gun and told me how to operate it, although I never used it in a combat situation. We were running for our lives and didn't look behind us. At one point, we were forced to leave behind our food supply.

The only time I fired the gun was when I accidentally pulled the trigger in a room full of people, scaring everyone to death. In that same room, I met Ferenc Szálasi, a Nazi leader in Hungary. He too was running for his life from the Russian air attack. He tightly held his wife and two small children in fear in the little house we were staying in as we traveled west. After the war, he was tried and executed for the war crimes he had committed.

No matter where we went, we saw signs of the war: houses were in ruins and people were moving from place to place trying to find safety.

We were soon in Austrian territory. As we walked I noticed dead bodies on the side of the road. They were wearing uniforms with stripes. I wondered who were they. Almost every mile we saw one or two in the ditch. Some even had a piece of meat in their hand. A few days later the mystery was solved. We discovered that they were German political prisoners who were being driven by prison guards. When they were unable to walk, they were shot and pushed into the ditch.

After marching for days, we went down a steep mountain road. It was difficult to keep the wagon on the right side of the road. At a sharp curve the horses could not hold the weight of the wagon, and it drifted to the left and into the other lane. Unfortunately, a German officer suddenly rounded the bend. We almost collided with his jeep, but he came to a screeching stop. Jumping from his car, he pulled out his revolver and shouted, "I will kill you, I will kill you, Hungarians dogs!"

We apologized for our "mistake," even though there wasn't anything we could have done differently since the roads were so curvy. He cursed and shouted more before finally leaving us alone.

We knew that we were on the wrong side of the road, but to call us "Hungarian dogs" was too cruel. We didn't start the war, nor did we cause it. It was Germany's fault! They were the guilty one! Our country was suffering because of their choices, but now they wanted to call us " Hungarian dogs." What unfair treatment!

A few days later our unit settled in at a small farm on a mountainside in Austria. Most of us wanted to try and reach the American-controlled territories. We knew that the war was on their side, and we had heard that the Americans were treating their prisoners with dignity. So we wanted to be in their occupied territories. But the lieutenant in our group said that we were not going any further. Our location was fairly isolated. We were high up on the mountainside, but we could see the valley below us.

One day a German soldier showed up in our camp. Swinging his machine gun around, he demanded that we give him one of our wagons and two horses. Our lieutenant said that we needed them. The two of them argued about who needed it most. Finally, the German got tired of arguing and decided to take action. He began to clear out the wagon, throwing our things onto the ground. Our officer commanded us to put our things back into the wagon. Because I was the closest to the wagon, I made the first move. He threw things out, and we threw them back in. This "game" went on for awhile until the German get tired of it. At the end of his rope, he pulled out his machine gun and shouted. We all froze. I looked to the lieutenant to see what he would do. He hesitated for a few seconds, analyzing the danger. Finally, he said, "Let him have it!"

I was very grateful because I feared that he would have killed a few of us, including me since I was closest to him, before we could have overpowered him.

We had nothing to do in camp except hang around. Out of boredom, I decided to venture down into the valley and see what was going on. On one occasion I heard gunshots between a German soldier and a group of Russians, but I was far enough away from the fighting to not be involved in the fray.

On another occasion in the valley, I almost lost my life. I was roaming around on the major road that ran through the valley looking for discarded items by the running

German soldiers when three Russian tanks showed up from the forest. I heard some noise, but I thought they were further away. When they emerged from the woods, I had nowhere to hide.

If I run, the soldiers on the tank will shoot me, thinking I did something wrong. If I stand still, I may survive, I thought.

So, I chose to stand still. The soldiers seemed to be looking straight ahead and pointing their machine guns forward as their tanks passed by me at a distance of only fifteen feet away. I believe God miraculously saved my life that day.

Soon after this, Germany and its allies surrendered. Because we were in a territory that had been conquered by Russia, we became captives of the Russian Army. We could not leave the area for the region was crawling with Russian soldiers rounding up the captives. Once we were all together, they made us march for days without food and water to an unknown destination. When we crossed into Vienna, the women in the city had compassion on us. As we passed through, they tried to give us bread and water. However, as we reached for the gift, a Russian solder on horseback whipped us back into line. A few days later we arrived at their prison camp. It was surrounded by three lines of barbed wire fence, and guarded with machine guns at every corner. From there, they transported captives to Siberia for hard labor. I waited for my turn to be shipped out, figuring that every day may be my last in Austria. There was little food; however, we survived. One time we discovered some soybeans in an attic in the camp, and we roasted the beans. It tasted delicious. Sadly, when the Russians discovered our "treasured food," they confiscated it from us.

We didn't have anything to do in the camp, so we talked and listened to each other's stories, hoping against hope that we would be released someday soon. Since I had so much free time, I made a hardwood chess set. I don't remember how I got the wood or what happened to my treasure when I was released from prison, but it helped pass the time.

As we all waited to see what our future held, sometimes guys got on each other's nerves. One guy in particular kept bothering me, pushing me and making nasty comments, until I couldn't take it anymore. I had avoided him for quite some time, but one day I had had enough. My brother and I were pretty good at wrestling. So when this guy "challenged" me to a fight, I accepted. I gripped him by the neck and threw him to the ground and then sat on his chest. He was so surprised that he could not do anything. I hit him until I felt that I had made my point. Then I stood up and walked away.

Quite a group of guys had gathered around to watch the fight, including my brother. After I walked away, the other guy got up off the ground and said, "He was lucky that I was on the ground; otherwise he would have gotten it!"

My brother responded, "I don't thinks so, friend!"

"Why not?" he questioned.

"You see, I was watching to see who the winner would be. If I thought he was losing, I would have stepped in."

"Why would you have helped him?" he asked.

"Because he is my brother!"

He didn't say anything. He just walked away.

After almost six months in captivity, a Russian officer called my brother and me into his office. Through a translator, he made a big speech. The piece that I remember is as follows: "You committed a great sin when you chose to fight against a great and peaceful nation. We should punish you for this crime. But the Great Russian Army, who victoriously defended its territory, is generous to you. As of today, we are letting you go free!"

I couldn't believe my ears! "We are letting you go free!" rang in my ears. It sounded like a dream. After spending months being confined in this horrible place, we were finally free! He gave us a certification of release, and my brother and I walked out of the prison camp. A few days later the rest of our group was set free. We had all survived the war!

Some of my family members were not so fortunate. Two of them lost their life in the war, one was carried home without legs, and two members came home very sick. War is cruel and confusing. Oftentimes many innocent people suffer and die.

I can hardly wait for the time when everything will be "clear" and eternal peace will reign in the kingdom of God.

Chapter 7

Meeting My Savior

Many people ask me why I am a Bible-believing Christian. And why I believe in God. Although I had been exposed to God as a child, it wasn't until after my release from the prison camp that I found God.

A few days after I was freed from the prison camp, my family was invited to a small prayer meeting in our village. My mother and I went. There was only a few people there, but their words were simple and full of love. They talked about God and His love. They also talked about Jesus Christ, who died for our sins on the cross of Calvary. They touched my heart. They were so delighted when I promised them that I would study more about these subjects when we got back to Budapest.

Within a few days we packed up our things and headed back to the capital. Once we were settled, my mother and I looked up the given address to the church that they had recommended. This church family also welcomed us with delight. We told them about our connection with the church in the village and that we wanted to know more about the Bible and Jesus Christ. I also expressed my desire to join the church. They told me that in order to be part of the church I needed to complete twenty-four lessons, which would teach me about the Bible and the beliefs of the church. I thought this was strange because I just wanted to accept Jesus as my Savior and be baptized into the church. The Bible teacher explained that I needed to know all the teachings of the Bible in order to be a member of the church. I could not understand it at the time, but later I was so grateful for those Christ-centered lessons. They were and still are the sure foundation of my faith.

Following is a short summary of those lessons, which molded my life and still shape it to this day. I discovered much joy as I studied God's Word.

I Am a Sinner

The first thing the Bible instructor explained to me was that I am a sinner and in need of a Savior (Rom. 3:23, 24; 6:17, 18). The Savior came to us as a human being to take away the sins of the world (John 1:29). In His life and teaching, He introduced the concept of salvation. He showed us His Father, who is also filled with love and compassion toward us (John 3:16). When Jesus finished His work on earth, He died on the cross in the place of man (Rom. 5:8). And although "the wages of sin is death, ... the gift of God is eternal life" (Rom. 6:23). If I confess my sins, God is willing to forgive me and give me a new life (Rom. 6:10, 11). The teacher taught me that in order to be a Christian I must be born again by "water and the Spirit" (John 3:5). God calls us to live a godly life by the indwelling Spirit of God and to be baptized by immersion (Rom. 6:3, 4).

There Is a God

After hearing about my need for a Savior and learning about God, I accepted Him right then and there. From that time on He was so real to me. He hears our prayers. You may ask how I know or what proof I have that God exists and cares about us, but when I look back on my life, I can see His hand of providence and protection. I know God is real, not only because of personal experience but also because of world history. The books of Daniel and Revelation outline the future events of the world and the end of time. The prophecies that God had Daniel and John record in the Bible have been fulfilled to the letter. He has all power and control of the universe.

David said, "The heavens declare the glory of God; and the firmament shows His handiwork" (Ps. 19:1). I have seen His handiwork on the screen of an electron microscope in the research laboratory where I worked. The structures, arrangements, functions and perfect relationships of our tissues in our bodies; the molecules, the single cell, tissues, organs and systems—they all work as a clock in unity and perfect harmony. All tell me of a wise and powerful God who designed our bodies. No wonder David said, "I will praise You, for I am fearfully and wonderfully made; marvelous are Your works, and that my soul knows very well" (Ps. 139:14).

He is a mighty God! He is not only the Creator of the universe, but He is my personal Friend. He is a loving God, and He is everything to me. He is my life; therefore, I love Him and believe in Him!

Bible and Its History

Next we studied about the Bible. The Bible means "collection of books." Where did it come from? Who wrote it? What does it say and do? Let me answer those questions

Meeting My Savior

and how it affected my life.

Further, I learned that forty men wrote the Bible over a time period of 1,600 years, inspired by the Holy Spirit of God. Moses was the first person to write a book of the Bible. He wrote about creation, the fall of man, and the provision of God to save humanity (Gen. 1; 2). He also wrote about the worldwide flood when God's judgment descended on an unrepentant and evil generation (Gen. 6). I learned that God called out a people, Israel, to represent Him by their works and life (Isa. 43:10). I excitedly read about the Ten Commandments, which God wrote in His own finger for all generations (Exod. 19:16; 20:1–17; Deut. 9:10, 11). The law represents His character, His mighty and unchangeable will for mankind.

I had struggled to make sense of the trials of life and the hate and destruction of war, but as I studied the Bible, everything became clear to me. The Bible held all the answers to life! The Bible tells us where we came from, where we are, and where we are going. It tells us how sin came into this world and how destructive it is if we ignore the Bible and its advice. God spoke to my heart through His written Word.

The Bible can change the life of a sinner and give him hope. It has power! The Word of God gives hope to this troubled world and to the weary soul. No other book can do it! So many people throughout history have ignored it or tried to destroy it, but this marvelous Book is still here and speaks to those who will humble themselves and believe.

Next we studied about the history of Israel and their sacrificial system. I learned that this ritual represented the coming Messiah who died on the cross for sinners, bringing the need for animals sacrifices to an end. As we studied history in light of the Bible, I read about the rising and falling of nations and the tremendous patience of a loving God.

Once we came the New Testament, I discovered the powerful message of the gospel as a fulfillment of Old Testament prophecy. The detailed life and work of Jesus as recorded in the Gospels documents the love of God and the gift of salvation that is freely given to all those who believe. The last Bible writer was John, the beloved disciple of Jesus. When we came to the book of Revelation, I marveled at the accuracy of the last events concerning world history, the final judgment of God, and the promise of Christ's return. I rejoiced in the promise of the new earth and new heaven. Jesus came to this earth for one reason: showing the Father's love to a fallen race and redeeming us so that we can live for eternity with Him.

I also learned that Jesus is in the heavenly sanctuary now, mediating for our salvation (Heb. 8:6; 12:24). Soon, He will come back to finish His redeeming work and take His people to His kingdom. The Old and New Testaments are in complete harmony.

I accepted all these biblical facts, and by His power, I am obedient to His requirements. I also do my best to share the saving knowledge that I know with others.

There Is a Creator

After reading the Creation story, I accepted the teaching that God created the world in six days. In fact, I took my newfound knowledge to my biology class years later when I moved to America. When the professor began talking about evolution, I raised my hand and asked to speak to him privately. He invited me forward to the board. Once standing in front of him, I said, "I am from Hungary. For ten years I listened to the same evolutionistic theory in that communist country. It is a disturbing experience to me that I am hearing the same thing in a Christian country. It is a well-known fact that evolution is just a 'theory' and not a proven 'fact.'" I continued, "There is another thing I would like to say."

I stepped to the board and made a vertical line from top to bottom. "At the left side of the line are the numerous scientists who believe and teach evolution. They argue among themselves as to the age of our world. The argument goes on and on about the time and stages of our 'development' in that process. There are many different viewpoints among them. The other side of the line displays only one biblical revelation, which says, 'In the beginning God created the heaven and earth.' It exists because He put it there. It is one explanation, one description, and one method. And God did it all! It is easier to believe in the Bible creation than the confusion on the other side. I believe in Creation instead of evolution. I will learn the evolutionary theories that you teach, but I can't believe in it!"

I read the unspoken thought on his face, *How dare you question my scientific knowledge!* Without a shadow of a doubt, I believe that a loving God created the world and set it into motion.

There Is a Savior

I thoroughly enjoyed studying about Jesus Christ, the Savior of the world. He is the center of the Old Testament as well as the New Testament. He is the "Alpha and Omega, the Beginning and the End ... who is and who was and who is to come" (Rev. 1:8). We read about the Savior within the first few pages of the Bible. Genesis 3:15 tells us about His mission and victory over Satan. Jesus is also portrayed in the last book of the Bible as the conquering "King of kings and Lord of lords" (Rev. 19:16).

The sacrificial offerings in the Old Testament pointed to the Redeemer of the world—the Messiah who would save the world from their sins. The Old Testament also portrayed God as the "Rock," which provided water for Israel in the wilderness to quench their thirst (Num. 20:11). He also safely led them through the wilderness for forty years (1 Cor. 10:1–3). He was the heavenly manna that fell every day and satisfied their hunger (Exod. 16:14–35).

Jesus said, "Whoever drinks of the water that I shall give him will never thirst. But the water that I shall give him will become in him a fountain of water springing up into everlasting life" (John 4:14). In addition, Jesus is our "bread of life" (John. 6:35).

Sadly, when the promised Messiah came, "His own did not receive Him. But as many as received Him, to them He gave the right to become children of God" (John 1:11, 12). And some day all those who believe in God will be rewarded with eternal life (John 3:16). I am ever thankful that I learned about Jesus Christ, the Savior of the world!

There Are Laws
As I studied, I learned that there are two basic laws: physical laws and moral laws. Both are eternal. If we violate any of these laws, we will reap the consequences. If you fall from a rooftop, willfully or accidentally, you get hurt or you may die because you have violated a physical law—the law of gravity. If you change the "structure" or "mechanism" of physical laws, you get disaster. (Think about the atomic bomb that was dropped on Japan.) There are laws everywhere. They are in cities and towns and schools and churches. Without them we cannot function.

This reminds me of an experience in New York City. For a time, my wife and I worked in downtown Manhattan. One night when we got in our car to head home, we discovered that all the stoplights were not working because there was a blackout in the city. No one knew whether to stop or go. Everybody tried to move at the same time, blocking each other with their cars. It was utter chaos. The usual thirty-minute drive home took more than two hours!

I learned that the Ten Commandments were given to us by God and that the first four talk about how we should worship God and the next six talk about our relationships with our fellow men. God gave us His laws to follow and grow in a relationship with Him; however, we cannot earn salvation because we perfectly follow the law. When we "look into the perfect law of liberty" (James 1:25), as into a mirror, and see ourselves as a sinner in need of Savior, then we have come to the place where we are willing to turn our life over to Jesus and follow His laws out of love and obedience for His commands. God's Word is clear—the law is there to help us control our behavior toward God and our neighbors.

When I surrendered my life to Him, He gave me the power to keep the law.

There Is a Message to Give
Jesus came to this world to offer salvation to anyone who believes in Him. As I grasped this concept, I was also taught that I was to share the good news of salvation with others as Jesus commanded one of the men He healed. "'Go home to your friends, and tell them what great things the Lord has done for you, and how He has had compassion on you.' And he departed and began to proclaim in Decapolis all that Jesus had done for him" (Mark 5:19, 20). The "good news" is that we are saved by His grace. Spreading the gospel is not only our responsibility but also our honor and joy as well. The world is in spiritual darkness. Many are without hope and discouraged. They need to hear about a loving God who sent His Son to save

us. We must tell them that there is a better way. They must know that Jesus is coming back soon to take us to His eternal kingdom. What a wonderful message to share!

As I learned about sharing the gospel message with the world, I read about God's remnant people (Rom. 11:5) who are called to proclaim the three angels' message (see Rev. 14:6–12). The first message is the "everlasting gospel" to the world—a call to "fear God and give glory to Him, for the hour of His judgment has come" (Rev. 14:7). The angel also calls everyone to worship the Creator. The second message proclaims that Babylon (confused religions) has fallen, because she has contaminated the nations with her wine (false doctrine). The third message warns of the judgment of God that will fall upon those who worship false gods and religions. They are very serious messages, and all have to decide whom they want to serve before Jesus returns.

What a joyous message we have to share with the world (Isa. 52:7)! I gladly accepted the call to serve God and tell others of His love.

There Is a Health Principle

I enjoyed learning new healthy practices and ways to take care of my body. Our physical, mental, and spiritual well-being are dependent on the laws of God, including the principles of health that He gave to man at creation. If we keep them, we will enjoy a long and healthy life. If we violate them, we may shorten our life. God created man to be perfect, without a trace of disease or deformity. Yet, life was given with a condition. If man obeyed God, he would live forever, but if he disobeyed, he would die (Gen. 2:16, 17).

Unfortunately, Adam violated this condition, and after leaving his home in the Garden of Eden, his body began to deteriorate, and he eventually died. With each passing generation, man lived shorter and shorter lives. Today if man lives 100 years or more, we call it a miracle.

If we are not thinking right, doing right, even eating right, we will shorten our life. Medical science proves that our mental and spiritual health affect our physical health. For example, I was the weakest and skinniest in my family. My sister and brother were strong and filled with vigor. Yet, both of them have passed away because they burned their "candles" at both ends. I lived a God-fearing and healthy lifestyle. In addition, I chose to become a vegetarian based on Bible principles and the research of medical science.

The Bible shows that Jesus was concerned about the physical health of the people he came in contact with, besides their spiritual well-being. The Bible says that He healed everyone in some villages (Matt. 4:23, 24; 8:16, 17; Luke 4:40).

There Is a Day of Rest
Then the teacher went on to point out the truth about the Sabbath, which is in the very center of the Ten Commandments (Exod. 20:8–11). The fourth commandment contains ninety-six words, the longest of the commandments. However, it is the most neglected of the ten, even though God has told us to "remember" it (verse 8). It is the Sabbath of the Lord (verse 10). It is not a "Jewish Sabbath," it is the Lord's Sabbath! We must keep it holy because He made it holy (verse 10).

All human beings need to rest in order to function properly. When God formed the world, He created a day of rest for humanity. He did three things with that seventh day (Gen. 2:1–3). "He rested" on it and called that day "Sabbath." God did not rest because of fatigue, but because He completed His work. God is never weary, rather He gives strength to the weak (Isa. 41:28, 29). God knows that we need rest and a day to remember Him; therefore, He created a day for us to spend time with Him and rest from our work. I learned that the Sabbath will also be celebrated in heaven, for not only is it a chance for us to spend time with God, but it is a memorial of His work at Creation (Isa. 66:22, 23).

I asked questions about why most Christians keep Sunday holy. Most churches say that because Jesus rose from the grave on Sunday that we are to celebrate His resurrection and go to church on Sunday. Yet, my teachers clearly showed me that there is no command in the Bible telling the early Christian church to switch the day of worship. This truth was completely new to me. Yet, I believed the Word of God, so I decided to keep the Sabbath and the rest of the nine commandments. It was not easy in a godless, communist society, but with God's help, everything is possible!

There Is a Second Coming

Jesus' second coming is the greatest hope of all of His followers. His return signals the beginning of eternal life for the redeemed. This belief is based on the very words of Jesus when He promised His believers that He would return. He said, "Let not your heart be troubled; you believe in God, believe also in Me. In My Father's house are many mansions; if it were not so, I would have told you. I go to prepare a place for you. And if I go and prepare a place for you, I will come again and receive you to Myself; that where I am, there you may be also" (John 14:1–3).

But before Jesus can return, I learned that He is working on our behalf in heaven (1 Tim. 2:5; Heb. 8:6; 12:24). His current work was foreshadowed by the work of the high priest in the Old Testament. Leviticus 16 provides details of the high priest's work on the Day of Atonement, a ceremony that took place once a year in which the high priest entered the Most Holy Place and pled for the forgiveness of the people. Jesus is pleading our case before His Father in heaven. When we confess our sins, Jesus pardons us and writes our name in the book of life.

Sheer joy will accompany Jesus' second coming when the dead in Christ will be resurrected and the righteous who are alive will join them in the clouds and go to heaven (1 Thess. 4:13–18). What a joyous event that will be!

Eternal Life Is Our Reward
With eagerness and excitement I learned about the gift of eternal life, which is the culmination of God's work and saving grace. Finally, the redeemed will have eternal life and will be reunited with God in heaven! I eagerly read about God's plans for the future in Revelation 21 and 22. The new heaven and new earth that God will create for us to enjoy will be beyond our wildest imaginations. There will be no more sorrow, pain, or death. In that shining city the glory of God will be the light for God's children. He will walk among us and visit with us. The tree of life and the river of life will be in the middle of the city for all to enjoy. God's throne will also stand in the middle of the city.

I thank God for His amazing grace and love. He gave His Son that we may not perish, but have eternal life. After studying the Bible and its truths, I decided to believe in God and His Word and take a stand to follow Him. As a result of these studies, I was baptized into the Seventh-day Adventist Church on December 23, 1945. From that time on, I walked with God, sixty-six years as of the writing of this book. God is still teaching me eternal values, and I am eagerly looking forward to His second coming and His eternal kingdom. I can hardly wait to see my loving Savior who died for me on the rugged cross of Calvary.

When I look back on my life, I can testify that God was with me from the very beginning of my life, although I did not know it at that time. He was there when I was born. He comforted us when my father died. He was there when I cried in my loneliness in the field. His hands were the ones who saved me from a watery grave. His angels protected my family and me when the bombs fell in Budapest. Yes, His tender care followed me when I ran from the war. He was the One who distracted the tank operators when I was standing alone on the road. When I worried about the outcome of my time in the prison camp, He provided for my needs and opened a way of release. He then guided my footsteps to a simple prayer meeting. He was the One who opened the treasures of heaven when I was instructed in His marvelous ways. What else can I say? Yes, my Friend has been with me throughout my eighty-four years of life. He blessed my wife and I when we moved to America. He provided for me to obtain an education, a good job, and a nice retirement. He has abundantly blessed us!

Chapter 8

Fire for My Lord

After my conversion I had a fire in my blood, and I looked for something I could do for my beloved Savior who had saved my life. Hungary was in shambles; yet everyone was thankful that the war was over. Having survived the war, many people were awakened to their need of a Savior, and a religious revival took place in our country.

My church emphasized that the devastation of the past few years was the result of evil ambition and was a sign of the end. We set out to warn the people. We conducted evangelistic meetings and called for repentance. With the help of some Americans, my church set up a printing shop and a publication department, and we began to print books and magazines. They organized a literature ministry and asked for volunteers to distribute the printed materials in the city.

I heard the call, and because of my love for the Lord, I volunteered to spread the good news of the gospel as a literature evangelist, or colporteur. When I showed up at the publishing department, the leaders welcomed me to the group of sixty workers. (Toward the height of our ministry, we reached close to 100 colporteurs.) There was a period of training in which we were taught what to say and how to introduce the books and magazines. We learned about the books we would be selling. Our leaders also told us of the hardship and trials we would experience. However, they encouraged us to remember that we were representing the God of the universe as His ambassadors. We memorized a precious Bible text found in Isaiah that has filled my heart with joy since the day I learned it. "How beautiful upon the mountains are the feet of him who brings good news, who proclaims peace, who brings glad tidings of good things, who proclaims salvation, who says to Zion, 'Your God reigns!'" (Isa. 52:7).

My leaders assigned me a territory and told me I would receive a partner. They promised to visit and see how we were doing as soon as possible. They gave me money for transportation, and I headed out by train. As I rode to my territory, many different questions came to my mind. *What will my territory be like? Who will my partner be? How will I do? What kind of people am I going to deal with, and how many will I reach for Jesus? Will I be able to earn enough to make a living?* Many other questions also crowded into my mind.

Fortunately, a peaceful feeling overtook my worries. *You put your will upon the work of God. He will take care of you and your work.* Looking back on those days, I can testify that He did richly bless my work!

My first territory was the Baja and Mohacs area in southern Hungary. My first partner arrived soon, but a few weeks later he quit. Another came, but he too left soon after he arrived. The work we were involved in was not easy. It felt like we were often "in the valley" instead of "on the mountaintop." The people we visited each day were not always friendly and many were not interested in our books. Within quick succession, three partners came and left. I became discouraged, but God had a plan. He brought me a strong and faithful partner who stayed with me for more than a year before he became a minister.

My spirits were definitely lifted when I found a man of God with whom to share the burden. Sometimes we had to walk for miles, but we would often sing aloud as we traveled. Many people bought our books and liked them. After reading them many discovered the truth of the Bible and accepted Jesus Christ as their personal Savior. This was what kept us going when we got discouraged.

One time I came to a home and was invited in. The young woman who asked me to come in was sick and in bed. I introduced my books to her, and she was more than happy to listen to me tell her about Jesus Christ. As we talked, she wanted to know if she could accept Jesus into her heart right then and there. I assured her that she could, and we both had prayer. After asking Jesus to forgive her and save her, she asked me if she could be baptized into my church. Sadly, she was very weak, and she died shortly after our visit. I praise God that she heard the message of Jesus' saving grace before she died. I believe I will see her in the kingdom of God when Jesus returns for His saints. These kinds of experiences gave us power to keep going, regardless of the difficulties we faced.

Of course, there were also difficult days. On one such day, it was late afternoon, and I had not sold any books. As I was walking along the street, a vicious dog charged me. In my fear, I throw my case of books at it. The dog jumped and ran away, but when my case landed on the ground, one side ripped completely open and my books spilled into the street. As I gathered my books from the dust, I asked God to forgive my impatience. I asked Him to give me some success. Praise God that He blessed me in the next hour, and a man purchased a few books from me that made up for my day's work.

Sometimes we ran into difficulties with the authorities. We had a permit to sell books and magazines, but some police found fault with my paperwork one time and arrested me. It was early afternoon when I accidentally went to a police station. The house was not marked, so I had no idea the authorities were behind the door. When the man opened the door, it turned out to be the police chief, and he told me that my papers were not in order and he would have to put me in jail. His associate escorted me to the next town, which was about four miles away, to lock me up. As I walked with the police officer, I talked to him about my work. I explained that I was on a peaceful mission to bring salvation to all people because I loved them as God loves them. He did not say a word to me; he just listened.

When we arrived at the jail, they locked me up. I was in prison for the rest of the day, overnight, and most of the next day. They did not give me any food or water. Fortunately, late the next afternoon they let me go with a warning to not work in their town.

At times we had difficulties with the local priests, especially the Catholics. Many cities and towns in our territory were very much controlled by the priests. Whatever they said was "holy," and people obeyed them religiously. We had to work fast. When we got to the door we informed people that we were representing Jesus Christ and our books contained the truth about the way of salvation. We encouraged them to read the Bible for themselves.

In one town the priest found out that we were going door to door, and the next Sunday the priest told his congregation from the pulpit that the "heretics are here in the town going house-to-house with their false teaching." He warned them not to buy any literature from us. For those who had already purchased books, he told them to burn them. Some heeded his advice and proudly torched our precious materials.

In another town we sold a lot of literature and invited the people for a special evangelistic meeting held by an Adventist minister. The response was so great that almost all the people of the town came to the meeting. However, a few minutes before the pastor started to speak, the priest of the town appeared and interrupted our meeting. He went right to the pastor and, with an unfriendly tone, asked, "Who gave you permission to come to my town and preach to my church members?"

"Jesus Christ!" answered the pastor.

The priest turned to the people and asked, "Who wants to leave the Catholic Church and follow this man?"

Of course, the people did not understand what was going on. They immediately said, "None of us!"

The same people who had come with a joyful and open heart to hear the sermon were now very hostile. We quickly left the town, for they were threatening violence toward us.

In the summer we liked to join our brothers for training and encouragement. We enjoyed studying together and sharing stories of God's providence and grace in the field. We welcomed the chance to listen to great speakers and spiritual leaders from our church. Besides spiritual nourishment, we enjoyed good, homemade food! Sometimes we did not have sufficient food, so it was a treat to be nourished in the physical sense.

In addition to the spiritual encouragement, the group also enjoyed fun events such as swimming and other outdoor activities. One day a cow wandered into our campground. We did not know where it had come from or who owned it. The camp manager, Pastor L., told us to lead her to a safe place until the owner showed up. A few hours later, still no one had showed up to claim the cow. It was evident that she was past milking time, so the request was made whether anyone knew how to milk the cow. Finally, someone volunteered, but milking the strange cow was not easy because she was nervous in a "strange place," and she ended up kicking the man. We were glad when the owner of the cow showed up and took her home.

The whole story was so funny that we decided to replay the events of the day in the form of a skit. We did such a good job that some people were falling off their chairs because they were laughing so hard.

I began working as a colporteur in 1946, and I continued in the work until 1950 when the communist government took over and confiscating our printing equipment and told us to stop distributing religious materials.

Chapter 9

My Sweetheart

In 1950 we entered into a difficult time in Hungarian history. The occupied Russian forces heavily influenced the government, and they curtailed all religious activities or completely stopped them. Many churches closed.

The government said, "Religion is the opium of the people, and they don't need it! God is just a theory, and the Bible is just a fairytale. We will control our lives, and by our effort, we will create a better world." These and similar teachings created a godless, atheistic society. Even today, sixty years later, there is still godlessness in Hungary. During this time, many lost their faith in God and the Bible.

Since I couldn't continue working as a colporteur, I began looking for other work. However, without a formal education, I had a hard time finding a job. After trying many places, I finally found a job in the city of Szekesfehervar. Once I relocated there, I joined a nice church with many young people. To my great surprise, among the young people was a beautiful girl of whom I wanted to get to know better.

My job in the city was to give out tools to maintenance workers in a textile refinery factory. This organization worked five days a week, but shortly after I began my employment with them, they announced a ten-day maintenance program. The institution stopped their regular work, and our shop was tasked with checking all the machines in every place during a ten-day period. They said that every maintenance worker had to work for the next ten days straight. I told them that I was a Seventh-day Adventist and would not work on Saturdays.

My boss said, "If you won't come in on Saturday, then don't come in on the following Monday." Just as quick as I had gotten a job, I lost it. When I went back for my remaining paycheck, I met the chief engineer who was a Jew. He had heard my story and was very sad that I had not come to him before I was fired because he could have helped me.

I prayed about my situation and looked into other job opportunities. Then I discovered that the city hospital was looking for help in the Pathology Department. I would be assisting the pathologist by moving the cadavers so that he could determine the cause of death. I shivered at the thought of touching dead bodies, but I was desperate to have a job, so I applied for it. They told me that I would be responsible for preparing the cadavers for the examination and assisting the doctor as he worked on them. They told me the job was six days a week. I told them that I was willing to learn and do the job but that I would not work on Saturdays. They told me they would discuss my request with the president of the hospital and get back to me.

The chief of the laboratories, the pathologist, and the president met and discussed my Sabbath request. The president was very friendly and supportive of my religious conviction. He listened to the arguments of the two doctors for half an hour. Then he said, "Please, gentlemen, find a way to solve this Sabbath question, and let the young man have the job."

At first it was not easy working with dead bodies, but after awhile I became accustomed to the job. As I assisted the pathologist, I learned about the anatomy of the human body. I also learned how to prepare specimens for histological examinations. As a result, this experience launched me into a career in the medical field and upon moving to the United States I obtained a steady job as an histology technician.

We worked on one to three bodies every day. I learned how to detect the cause of death by watching and listening to my boss. I became so proficient at my work that my boss occasionally let me take the lead for a case. He simply supervised my work and signed off on my findings.

My boss and the chief doctor of the laboratories were the professional authorities in criminal cases in the city, and I was their right-hand man. Many times we were asked to go to different cities and towns to investigate criminal cases. On one occasion a young man was found dead in a well filled with rotting dead animals. Foul play was suspected, but our investigation proved that the fumes from the dead animals killed him. It was determined that he had gone to the well to retrieve a dead pig that had recently been thrown in and use it for food. But he had died in the process.

Through this job I discovered that I really enjoyed science and medicine. My interest in religion also remained strong as I grew in these other areas of knowledge. I attended church faithfully every week and continued to strengthen my walk with God. An added benefit of going to church was that I got to see the pretty girl that I had noticed the first time I had attended church. I took advantage of every opportunity to get to know her. She was a faithful and well-respected member of the congregation.

After spending time with her and observing her, I determined that I loved her. And I worked up the courage to ask her to marry me. I thought she would say "yes," but to my surprise, she said "no!" I thought my world was going to collapse. I decided not to talk to girls anymore!

I decided to forget my "disappointment" and concentrate on my job and pursue a formal education. Because I was enjoying my work in the medical field, I decided that I wanted to become a physician.

I soon discovered that going to school was hard work! I was still working full time and taking classes in the evening. I then had to come home and study late into the night. It took all my time and energy. I did not have time for girls! Or so I thought!

Even though I was so busy, I couldn't forget the girl I loved. I still saw her every Sabbath in church. She sang solos and got involved in the other activities at the church, so I couldn't avoid her. I still loved her with all my heart. How could I forget such a beautiful girl who was constantly before my eyes? After many months I approached her and asked her to reconsider her decision. To my disappointment, she said no again. I was frustrated and upset at her. *Who does she think she is?* I thought. *Is she a queen waiting for a prince to marry her?*

I continued to bury myself in work and school, hoping to forget about her. Unfortunately, all of the stress that I was under led me to develop an ulcer, which left me in constant pain. It was so severe that I had to spend a few weeks in a sanitarium. The treatments that I received helped somewhat. But then I was faced with the challenge of catching back up on my studies. I managed to get up to speed on every subject except math. At the end of the year, the professor flunked me, which meant that I had to spend the summer making up the class. Fortunately, I did well the second time around and was able to advance to my fourth year. (In Hungary they called it higher education, but in the United States, the program I completed would be equivalent to high school.)

During this time I lived in the basement apartment of the church with a few other young men. We highly appreciated the help that our church provided without charge. There was a time when there were ten of us living in the basement. We helped each other and encouraged each other to remain true to our beliefs. On Sabbath we enjoyed a variety of spiritual activities, starting with Sabbath School, which was a highlight of our week. On the other six days, we faithfully studied the lesson so that we could share our thoughts with others. I was always anxious to hear what the others had to say on the same subject. After Sabbath School we listened to the Christ-centered sermons by our pastor or a guest speaker. In the afternoon we had a meeting just for young people; however, young and old attended. We all supported each other and grew in our faith together.

One day at church I was in for a big surprise. A girl from the congregation who knew of my marriage proposal approached me and said, "Did you know that she has changed her mind about you?"

"No! I did not know that," I said. "How do you know that she did?"

"Just trust me and ask her again," she said. "This time she may say yes."

I did not have much hope that she had changed her mind, but I decided that it was worth a try. After the youth meeting, I asked her if I could accompany her home. To my surprise, she said, "If you feel like it, that's OK with me!" That gave me hope!

She lived about thirty minutes from the church. I don't remember what we talked about, but when we reached our destination, I worked up the courage to ask her again. "Elizabeth, will you marry me?" I looked at her face and waited for the answer.

Than she made two statements of which I will never forget. "Yes, Alex, I will marry you! But you must promise me that from now on you will be more serious."

You see, all her life she had been "serious." She didn't like it when young people talked silly or joked around. But I was a fun-loving guy who liked to joke around sometimes. I took life easy. Of course, when I heard that, I said, "Yes, Elizabeth, from now on I will be more serious!" After sixty years of marriage, I think she is still waiting for the fulfillment of that promise.

A few days later we held an engagement ceremony, and one year later we got married on December 5. What a wedding! I thought the entire city came to see us. My boss was the best man, and the Police Department provided a car for our transportation. The church was full of relatives and friends. The preacher got excited when he saw the crowd and he began to preach a long sermon, but it was beautiful, and we joyfully remember our special day.

Chapter 10

Separation

A few weeks after the wedding my wife felt somewhat unusual, so she went to see a doctor. After he conducted an exam, he told her she was pregnant. I was surprised, but she was upset!

"We haven't been married that long. I don't want to be pregnant already," she said. "We need so many things, and now we have a baby on the way! You should have been more careful!"

"Yes, yes, honey, I know!" I said. "But it will be OK."

She certainly didn't think so. After having a few heated conversations, I suggested that we go see the pastor. We shared with him our situation, and he happily replied, "It is wonderful that you are having a child!" His words did not comfort her.

I then made an appointment with a skilled and well-known physician at the hospital where I worked who specialized in obstetrics. After examining my wife, he said, "Ms. Fulop, you are a beautiful and healthy woman. You should be thankful that you going to have a healthy child.

I wish you much happiness with your child!" After this appointment my dear wife had peace of mind and accepted the fact that we were going to have a child.

After nine months of waiting, we welcomed a baby girl into the world and named her Erika. She was the most beautiful girl we had ever seen in the world. Both of us were immediately in love.

Shortly after Erika's birth my ulcers started to act up. It was so painful that I could hardly stand it. I made an appointment to see a surgeon in the hospital. He was a well-known and God-fearing man. He looked at my medical records and discovered that I had many ulcers on the duodenum and its vicinity. He turned to me and said, "Alex, they look bad. Let's take them out." Within a few days he operated on my ulcers, and my pain ceased. Three days after the surgery I felt so great that I drank some fresh grape juice, but this almost killed me. I had such severe cramps in my abdomen that I was rushed to the hospital. Fortunately, I didn't do any long-term damage. They scolded me a little bit and gave me some medication. Praise God the medicine worked, and the next day the cramps were gone, and I felt great again.

It was now 1956, a famous year in Hungarian history. A group of students in Budapest presented a request for freedom of the press and religion. Then more and more citizens jumped on the bandwagon and demanding more rights until a full revolutionary movement was swelling to send the Russians home. It was more than the Kremlin could tolerate. They decided that if they let Hungary go that all the other countries they occupied would demand the same thing. This would result in them losing all their influence and benefits of those countries. So they decided to fight back.

In one great push, they brought back their mighty forces. Ground troops and tanks descended on every big city and opened fire upon the freedom fighters. After a few weeks of heavy fighting, they squashed the Hungarian uprising. Many Hungarians as well as some Russian died in the fighting. Many people were also arrested and imprisoned or killed. These were very sad days for our country's history.

After the fighting I heard a story that brought great joy to my heart and reminded me of God's protection. A Russian soldier who had accepted Christ and become a Seventh-day Adventist had drifted away from the church before the fighting broke out and was living a life without God. Now he was fighting in a big battle in the streets of Budapest. He was in a leading vehicle with a military officer. Shots were coming from every direction, and his fellow Russians soldiers were dying by his side. Tanks were being taken out around him. He feared for his life, and then he remembered God. He bowed his head on the steering wheel and in honest repentance cried out for forgiveness. If he was going to die, he wanted to die knowing that God forgave him and that he would be in the kingdom of God.

Than a miracle happened. Not a singular bullet hit their vehicle, even though shots were ringing out all around them. The officer asked him, "What is happening?" He explained that he used to go to church but had left and now asking God to forgive him. The officer was amazed. They survived the battle, and soon after this young soldier went home and returned to church. I took courage in this story, knowing that God watches over his children from all nationalities.

After the fighting, what limited freedom was stripped away. Under communist rule, religious freedom was a foreign concept. Many people were put onto a "black list." During the first stage of the revolution, I discovered that I was on that list because of my religious conviction.

I feared for our religious freedom and the ability to earn a living, so I told my wife that I thought we should move to America. She was stunned! She expressed her fear of the "unknown." I tried to reason with her that anything would be better than how we were living now. She could not see my viewpoint. Finally, in her anger and frustration, she said, "Go! Don't come back. I don't want to see you anymore!" These words were hard to swallow, but I did what she said. I told my mother-in-law that I was leaving and that when I prepared a place for them, I would send for Elizabeth and Erika. My brother and my sister-in-law and her future husband felt the same way as I did, so they prepared to leave with me. We felt confident that we would do better in the West.

However, there were still hurdles to overcome. It was not easy getting out of the country because the Russian forces were closing the borders. We picked an area of the country that we thought was still free, and we headed in that direction. Sometimes we walked, and sometimes we took the train. It took us a few days to reach our destination. Along the way we slept in open fields, in barns, or in peoples' homes who sympathized with us. When we arrived at the border, we found thousands of other Hungarians like us who were trying to flee the country. Unfortunately, they shut the border down to stop the flow of people. We tried to go though, but failed. Then we found out about a person who knew the area and was willing to help us cross.

The next evening we followed him to an extremely strange area. It appeared to have been a swamp, but it was now dry. The ground was as hard as a rock. After a long walk in the dark, we reached the ramp of a channel. The guide stopped and told us, "Go up the ramp and a couple hundred yards away, you will find a bridge that leads to Austria." We paid our fee and headed for the bridge, dreaming of freedom. But our dream was "interrupted."

To our surprise, there were about a hundred or more people standing near the bridge. They appeared to be in some type of trouble. Women and children were crying. Everyone feared that the Russian forces would show up any minute. The rumbling sound of tanks in the distance did not help us either. When we got closer, we asked, "Why you are here? Why are you not crossing the bridge?"

"Don't you know that the bridge was destroyed by the Russian forces just a few days ago?" they asked. Now I understood why our guide how not accompanied us all the way. We were so close, yet so far away from freedom.

Joseph, my future brother in-law, and I decided to investigate the area. It was about two o'clock in the morning and quite dark, but we still looked around to see if there was any hope of crossing the river to the other side. We went down to the edge of the water and found big pieces of lumber all over the place. Some floated in the water while other pieces hung from the remains of the bridge. We were delighted to discover that with these large pieces of lumber we could build a single bridge across the river. Within a few minutes we had finished the task of building the bridge, so we went and told the group to come down to the edge of the water and cross the bridge one at a time while holding tightly to their children. Miraculously, everyone crossed to the other side without a problem.

Once safely on the other side, we saw lights in the distance and people moving around. I told everybody to lie down until we could find out who they are. We were not exactly sure where the border was. We asked a young man to crawl toward the light and determine if the people were of Russian or Austrian descent. Within a few minutes, he waved for us to join him. We were all relieved to find out that the people were our Austrian neighbors. They welcomed us with hot drinks and kindness.

  I was extremely grateful to be safely in Austria, and I praised God for his deliverance and for the kind people of Austria who took me and my fellow countrymen in during our time of need.

Chapter 11

Entering My New Country

From the Andau Bridge in Austria we were transported further into the country in many different vehicles. A bus loading up some people, while my family and I climbed into a large wagon pulled by a truck. The wagon was full of straw, giving us a more comfortable ride. I sat near the edge, and in order to hold on as we jostled along, I stuck my left hand outside the wagon and grasped hold of the wooden slates that made up the sides.

As we traveled on the bumpy road, I thought about all that had transpired, especially my last moments at home. The last words of my wife and my sweet, little girl came to my mind. Deep down in my heart I had a strange feeling. *Will I see them again? Will they be able to come when I send for them? Did I do the right thing, leaving them behind?* I had tried to convince her to come with me, but she did not trust me enough to venture into the "unknown." I tried to understand her feelings, but I had an urge to go. I stepped out in faith, thinking that somehow, someway everything would be OK, that God would work everything out in the end.

As I was deep in thought, the truck suddenly veered off the road and down an embankment to avoid hitting another vehicle. Unfortunately, the wagon tipped over, sending all of us flying. Some people flew over me and out of the wagon, while others fell on me. My left arm was crushed under the wagon, and the loosened straw covered me completely.

"Help!" I called. My brother and some of the other passengers cleared away the straw and tried to pull me out. "Please don't do that!" I cried. "My arm is pinned under the wagon!" My brother, realizing what had happened, called for help and about fifteen men rushed to lift the wagon, releasing my severely injured arm.

I was in a lot of pain. I figured that I had broken something. A taxi took me to the nearest town with two other people who had been injured in the crash. There I met the rest of my family. The emergency workers told me that I needed to go to the hospital to receive treatment of my injuries. My family wanted to come with me to avoid being separated in a foreign country where we didn't speak the language, but the authorities told us that only those who were injured could go to the hospital.

Little did we know when we parted that we would not see each other for two months, despite attempts to track each other down, and that when we would be reunited, we would be in America.

Once I arrived at the hospital, the doctor examined my arm, and much to my surprise, nothing was broken. I only sustained severe bruises. They put my arm in a sling and made me stay for two days so they could observe my arm and make sure it was healing properly.

Upon my release, they asked me where I wanted to go. "To the SDA Center in Vienna!" I said. They looked it up, and than they put me on a train with written directions.

Not knowing the language, it was a miracle that I made it to my destination.

I reached the Adventist Church's headquarters in Vienna and found hundreds of refugees waiting for help. When the president of the Austrian Union saw my bandaged arm, he pointed to a chair and told me to take a seat. Within half an hour, I was connected to a Hungarian-speaking family who took me into their home and provided food and shelter for me.

The next day I located the refugee center and told the worker that I wanted to go to America. "Sorry, sir," one of the interpreters said, "the quota to America is already full. There are many openings to other countries, such as England, France, Italy, Argentina, Brazil, and Australia. But we can't place any other people on the list for America."

When I heard his lists, I panicked. I had no idea where my family was or if they had been told the same thing. Before we were separated, we had agreed to go to America, but I had no way of knowing whether they had changed their plans. As I considered my options, the man could tell I was torn, and he said, "Everybody wants to go to America. If you really insist on going there too, than wait awhile. We think America will vote again soon and allow another twenty thousand refugees into the country." This gave me some hope and peace.

Of course, waiting is hard to do, especially when you don't know how long you will have to wait. Uncertainty is a horrible thing! And the longer I waited, the more I questioned whether my decision was a good one or not. Weeks passed and I heard nothing!

It was near the end of December, right before Christmas, that I went into the office to see if they had heard anything. The man smiled at me and said, "I have good news! The president gave approval allowing another twenty thousand refugees to enter America."

"That is wonderful! Thank you, God," I said.

"Give me your ID, and I will process it," he said. "Please check in from time-to-time to know what day the trains will take you to the shore. An American troop carrier will then transport you to the United States."

I thanked him and told him that I would check back. Within a few days I boarded a train to the coast where I got on the ship that took me to my new home. I made myself comfortable on the ship and waited. The days crept by with little or no movement. Every day more refugees arrived and boarded the ship. I wasn't sure when we would be setting sail, but in the meantime, I enjoyed the food provided in the cafeteria. I was accustomed to simple meals, maybe one meat, one vegetable, one potato, and one desert. I had never seen so much food or so many selections in my life.

Christmas came and went without any news. The New Year arrived, and we still sat in the harbor. We finally received word that we were waiting on a few other people to arrive. We had to have at least two thousand on the ship to sail. Then, on January 4, we set sail. It was a wonderful feeling to be headed to our final destination. Of course, our "good feelings" didn't last long. Once we hit the open water, most of us became seasick. It felt as if our ship was just a toy boat in the bathtub. It was tossed up and down by the waves. We could not eat. Some became so sick that after the eleven-day voyage they had to be carried off the ship on a stretcher.

About three days later we noticed that the water was smoother. "What is happening?" we asked. We went up to the deck and saw some islands in the distance. "Where are we?" we asked.

"Those are the Islands of Azure," a more informed man said.

Oh how I wished that the water would stay this calm for the rest of the trip! But we soon left the sheltered shores of Azure and headed back into open water. Shortly after that the captain of the ship informed us that he was trying to avoid a big storm by navigating the ship south. Even with his efforts, we caught the tail end of it, and the rolling of the ship grew worse. Day and night we went up and down. I thought it would never end. Fortunately, it did come to an end—after eleven days we arrived in New York City.

The captain wanted to show us the Statue of Liberty, the great symbol of freedom, but it was so foggy that we could not see it. Upon reaching the port, we disembarked and boarded buses that took us to Camp Kilmer, an old military base in New Jersey. There were already thousands of people there. The first thing we had to do upon arriving at the base was go through a health screening. I figured I would breeze right through, but after the examination, they told me I had a questionable spot on my lung. "Lord," I prayed, "I am here in this free country, and now I may be facing the dreaded disease—tuberculosis. Now what will I do?" All kinds of negative thoughts ran through my mind. They told me I had to complete some additional tests. They put a tube down my throat—I thought I would choke!—and ran some other tests. After a few days, they finally said I was healthy, and my lung was OK.

In the meantime I learned that my family was living right there in New York City and were doing well. Soon a pastor arrived and took me out to start a new life in the country of my dreams.

Chapter 12

The Miraculous Reunion

Shortly after receiving a clean bill of health, a pastor picked me up at the camp and took me to find a job. Everything was so new and different. The hardest part was not knowing the language, but God helped me to adapt and quickly learn how to live in my new home.

Because I had experience working in a laboratory, within a few weeks I had a job in the Anatomy Department of one of the medical schools in New York City. Yet, at the same time I had a desire to go to collage. I looked at my options.

Meanwhile I met a woman at church whom I knew from Hungary. She was the wife of the head of the publishing department in Budapest. I told her that I wanted to further my education, and she helped me get into a school in Massachusetts. Within a short period of time, I quit my job and moved to Massachusetts with another young man to attend the college. Classes had not started yet, but we wanted to become familiar with the school and find part-time jobs.

To our surprise, after we arrived we got a letter from the pastor who sponsored us requesting that we appear before the church board and confess of our "sins." We were not sure what our "sins" were, but being respectful young men, we traveled back to the church, which was 150 miles away from the college.

During the meeting, the board demanded that we should "confess or sins." We asked them "what sins" they were talking about, but they wouldn't answer us. They simply said, "You see, brothers and sisters, they are so blind that they don't see their sins!" Because we were unsure of what they wanted us to do, we left the meeting and headed back to school. We thought that would be the end of the story, but we were mistaken.

Less than a week later the school principal called us into his office and told us that we had to leave the school. We were shocked. He didn't tell us the reason, but we had a good guess, figuring the pastor was upset that we hadn't "confessed our sins," and he was punishing us.

After leaving his office, we determined that we had four choices: 1) Tell everybody of their evil actions and defend our innocence; 2) leave the church because of our frustration with its spiritual leaders; 3) organize another church that is based on honesty; or 4) leave the situation in the Lord's hands and trust Him to work things out for our good. We chose the fourth option, and in the end, God turned everything around for our good.

Following the principal's request, we left the school and moved to the nearby city of Worcester. Both of us got a job. I as a histology technician, and my friend as a dental technician, which were our trades in Hungary. We also joined the local church and were warmly received. One year later we both received a good recommendation, and we both enrolled back at the college that had sent us packing the year before. God is good! He always cares for His children. Praise His holy name!

In addition to classes, I worked at two jobs to support myself. I would draw blood from 6:00–8:00 a.m. at the Worcester City Hospital, attend classes from 9:00 a.m.–noon, and then work from 1:00–5:00 p.m. counting cells in another laboratory. At suppertime I helped feed patients in a nursing home in exchange for room and board. In the late hours of the evening, I studied for my classes.

It was hard work studying for my classes and learning English at the same time, but God gave me the strength I needed. Of course, my family situation still greatly disturbed me. I missed my wife and daughter. After getting settled in America, I sent her a letter. She responded. But our first few letters back and forth contained heated words. We both blamed each other for our current situation. She argued that I had left them, and I argued that she had not been willing to come with me. We went back and forth. When we both calmed down and changed our attitude, we began to repair our relationship.

After corresponding for a while, she agreed to come to America to be with me. I tried all avenues to get them there. I wrote a letter to President Eisenhower. The U.S. government expressed sympathy, but they inform me that the Hungarian government would not let them leave. I asked churches in Austria and Hungary for help, but no one offered me any solutions. The only thing I could do was hope and pray, which I did a lot of!

Many people in my new home knew of my troubles. Some advised me to get married because I was never going to see my wife again. Others encouraged me to hold on and be faithful to Elizabeth and trust God to bring them to America. I chose to remain faithful to my wife and pray that God would work a miracle and reunite us.

I tried to forget my troubles by focusing on my schoolwork and doing some missionary work. On the weekends I usually went to a nearby cemetery to pray. It was a quiet place, and nobody disturbed me. One day I prayed, "Lord, how long do I have to wait? I know it was a mistake for us to separate. You know our situation. This separation is hard for her, as well as for me. Please help us!" I prayed.

Meanwhile, I tried to financially support them. I sent a large amount of money through the "black market." I had connections with a Hungarian lady who lived in Africa but had money in Hungary. I sent her money, and she had her people give my wife Hungarian currency. It was a risky business, but I took the risk. The woman was an honest person and did not disappoint me. The value of the dollar was so high at that time that when my wife got the amount it was equal to one year of my salary.

I sent her what I could, but I also had to pay for my education. She understood the situation and ended up getting a job at a textile refinery. It was not easy for her. But she was a hard-working woman, and she was faithful too. She was a beautiful women, and many men trying to approach her. One man was especially aggressive, and she hit him on the back. After that warning, he never bothered her again.

In regards to the opposite sex, my life was not any easier. I was surrounded by beautiful college girls, and it was hard not to be lonely and long for a companion. One time I wanted to ask a girl to a social because I didn't want to be alone. However, I asked her brother for advice before speaking with her. We were good friends, and he told me, "Alex, I wouldn't do that!" I thanked him for his advice, and I didn't ask anyone to accompany me.

The years kept slipping by, and I did not see any chance of our little family ever being reunited. Then, after five years of waiting, as I was praying in the cemetery one evening, pleading for the Lord to forgive our past mistakes and bring us back together again, I received an answer. I opened my Bible to Matthew 7:7 and put my finger on the text and read it aloud, "'Ask, and it will be given to you; seek, and you will find; knock, and it will be opened to you.' Here are Your word, Lord! You said we should ask, and You will give it to us. I claim Your promises! Please, answer my prayer! It is too hard for me to hold on any longer. Please, open the door for them! Lord, hear my prayer!"

Then I stopped and waited. I looked toward heaven. I did not hear a word from God. I did not receive verbal assurance that God had heard my prayer, but something happened in that quiet cemetery. My troublesome soul quieted down, and a heavenly peace filled my soul. Somehow I felt that within my heart my prayer had been answered. I did not see any visual evidence, but I felt that something would happen.

A few days later I met the president of the collage on campus. He was a wonderful, spiritual man who was always interested in the students and their problems. He was familiar with my situation. "How are things going, Alex?" he asked.

"Nothing new!" I said.

"Any news from your wife?" he continued.

"Nothing so far," I said.

"Come to my office and let's offer a special prayer for them," he suggested.

Once in his office, we knelt down to pray. He prayed first and asked God to intervene on my behalf. After he finished, I had a short petition. I felt that the Spirit of God was in that room. When we got up from our knees, he asked, "What would you think if I wrote to the Hungarian government and asked them to let your family come to the States?"

It touched my heart that he not only prayed for us but also was willing to go the second mile. I hesitated with my answer, thinking that a communist president would not be willing to do anything for a man who illegally left the country. I expressed these thoughts to him. "But on the other hand," I concluded, "we don't have anything to lose if you write the letter! I would greatly appreciate that!"

He didn't share the contents of the letter with me, but whatever he wrote brought about powerful results! A few weeks later a student approached me with a letter in his hand. "This letter came to President Reynolds," he said. "It is from the office of the Hungarian president. Dr. Reynolds does not understand it because it is written in Hungarian. But he is sure it is about you, because your name is in it. He believes it contains good news."

Why he felt it contained good news is still a mystery to me! I pulled the letter out and began reading. "Dear Mr. Reynolds, the president's office of the Hungarian government wants you to know that your petition concerning Elizabeth Fulop and her daughter's release has been granted!" It was signed by the secretary of the Hungarian president.

I couldn't believe my eyes! Our prayers had been answered! The messenger saw my face change and asked, "What does it say? We all want to know what it says!"

"They are coming!" I shouted. "The Hungarian government has given my wife and daughter permission to leave Hungary." I felt as if I was dreaming; tears of joy ran down my cheeks. I excitedly told everyone I met that my family could leave Hungary. Everybody who had prayed for us praised the Lord with me. My friends and church family made plans to throw a big welcome party for them when they arrived. I was the happiest man on earth.

A few days later I received a letter from my wife confirming that they could leave the country and asking me to send her money for the airfare, because there was a time limit for them to leave the country.

The big day finally arrived. I had to go to New York City to pick them up. Two other Hungarian students from the school also came with me. We decided to arrive a few days earlier, and I was glad we did because we had hardly made it fifty miles when my car broke down. "What will we do now?" we asked each other. Fortunately, a Hungarian friend in the city came and picked us up. My sister-in-law and her husband waited for us in New York. Everybody was so excited! We could hardly wait for them to arrive.

The time finally came when we all went to the John F. Kennedy Airport. We arrived early so that we could see the plane land. After five years of waiting, they were almost home! I cannot describe the feeling I had in my chest.

After the plane landed, we anxiously watched the terminal so that we could see them disembarking. My eyes were riveted to the area. I saw a little girl running around with a beautiful doll hanging in her hand. "That's my little girl, Erika," I shouted. "I sent her that doll a few years ago."

I could not hold in my emotions anymore. I ran down the corridor, passed the custom's officer. When I reached my wife, I threw my arms around her and held her close. I didn't want to ever let go of her again! The custom's officer just looked at us, not fully understanding that we hadn't seen each other in so long. I apologized and tried to explain, "They are my family, and I haven't seen them in five years. They just arrived from Hungary, and they do not understand English. I am here to help them." After we presented their papers, they were free to enter the country. Once cleared, we walked out together, my beloved sweetheart and my little darling. This was one of the greatest miracles of my life! When we were outside, I held her again, tight to my heart!

Later, Elizabeth told me the details surrounding their permission to leave the country. A high police officer delivered the permission to her home, but since it was Sabbath and she wasn't home, the officer went to the church. However, she wasn't there either because she was with the young people visiting another church. Since he couldn't find her, the officer told the people at the church that she was supposed to go to the Police Department for an "important piece of mail." When she went to pick up the "important piece of mail," she was surprised to see that she could leave the country. The one stipulation was that she would have to give up her Hungarian citizenship. When she went to the American consulate for more papers, they were surprised that she was able to go to America. They said, "No one can leave Hungary at this time, but you have been granted permission to leave." She knew very well that it was the hand of God that had worked this miracle on our behalf.

Chapter 13

Life Together

After celebrating for a few days in New York City, we headed back to Worcester. Once we were alone, we sat down and discussed what we should do next, including what I should do about my schooling. Although I had been taking classes for three years, I had only finished about half the credits I needed to obtain a degree in theology and graduate. The language barrier had definitely slowed me down. As we talked, Elizabeth shared with me that she was not comfortable being a minister's wife. She wanted to live a quiet life, and she knew that that was impossible for a pastor's family. She also expressed her concern over my inability to deal with stress and the fact that running a church is a very stressful job. After talking, we decided that we would wait awhile and see what the Lord had in mind.

I had experience in histology, and the Mason Research Institute in Worcester was looking for somebody in that field. It was a supervisory job that required leading four to six technicians in a research laboratory. I applied for it, and by God's grace, I got the job. Another blessing of this job was that the owner, Dr. Mason, was Jewish, so having Sabbaths off was never an issues.

The research lab tested the affects of viruses, bacteria, drugs, as well as stress on different animals. The experiment results on the tissues came to us already labeled and were in fixatives, a chemical substance. We filed them and left them in a solution-filled machine called a technikan overnight. The next morning the tissues were ready to place into a sectioning medium called paraffin. After they cooled, the tissues in the paraffin were cut with a sharp knife into thin sections, placed on a labeled slide, and stained with eosin and hematoxylin. The tissue slides were then examined. My job was to ensure that the process went smoothly, that the machines were working, and that the research was conducted in a timely manner.

Soon after getting settled and me accepting the job, Elizabeth became restless. She also wanted to work and support our family. She applied for a job at the same institution and was hired to work in my department as a technician. Within a few weeks she mastered the techniques needed for the job. To avoid any appearance of favoritism, I expected more work from her than the others. She worked without complaint.

Our daughter was seven years old at the time, and we desired to send her to our Adventist elementary school. Unfortunately, the school was on the other side of the city, and she had to take two buses to get there. Because of our jobs, we couldn't drop her off, so we asked her if she could ride the buses by herself. She was a brave and courageous girl, and she assured us that she would be fine. Elizabeth took her to school the first day and showed her the route. And from that day on she got to school on her own. Of course, because of her age, we worried about her safety. We constantly prayed that God would protect her while she traveled to and from school.

One day when she got home she told us that a man had followed her after she got off the bus. We were alarmed! We didn't know who he was or what his intentions were. I decided to take a day off of work and follow behind Erika to see if the man appeared again. Sure enough, the man followed her again, and I followed both of them. At the right time, I approached him and asked him what he was doing. Only the good Lord knows what was really on his mind. We praise God that He protected her and that we stopped him in time. After that encounter, he left our daughter alone.

For the next three years my wife and I worked at the research center together. We enjoyed our work and managed to get by on what we earned. However, Elizabeth missed her family and desired to live closer to her sister, Anna, who was in New York City. They had two sons now, and Elizabeth longed to get to know them. I thought her desire was unrealistic because we had steady jobs, but I decided to pursue the idea and see if God opened any doors.

I wrote a letter to a doctor I knew in the city. I told him my background and where I was currently working. I then asked him if he knew of any job openings in my area of expertise. He responded that he would look into it and call me in a few days.

Dr. Z. called back as he promised. "We have a job for you at New York Medical College. But there is a condition," he continued. "You have to learn electron microscopy."

Electron microscopy is similar to histology in that both deal with examining tissue. In histology, technicians work with light sources to see the results on the specimen, and the highest magnification is 2000X. In electron microscopy the magnification is much greater because of the wavelength of the electrons. The offer sounded very good to me, and I was excited to learn a new skill, so I accepted the job.

As I was working out the details about my new job with Dr. Z., Elizabeth came to my mind, and I decided that it couldn't hurt to ask him if he knew of a job for her as well. He was a kind man who liked to help people, especially Hungarians because his wife was also from Hungary. I told him that she was my best technician at the research center, and he told me that he would look into finding her a job too. A few days later he called back and offered her a job as well, a job she enjoyed for thirty-two years.

After obtaining jobs we were convinced that the Lord had opened the way for us to move and continue working in the medical field. Within a few weeks of accepting Dr. Z.'s job offers, we said goodbye to our friends in Worcester and moved to New York City, the city I had arrived in back in 1957.

Chapter 14

Relocating to New York

New York is a huge city with millions of people living there. It is a busy and sometimes dangerous city, but we were happy to follow where God was leading.

Upon getting settled, we joined a gospel-loving church. Elizabeth loved her job. Her boss, a chairman of the laboratories, appreciated her work. She did histology work at first, but later became his secretary. I, too, enjoyed my new job. It was very challenging learning a new skill, but the world of electron microscopy was fascinating.

Electron microscopy had just become a tool in the medical field, so we were exploring new territory. Electrons are created by high-temperatures on a cathode filament in a vacuum. Than the electrons are sent through a hole on an anode plate and modified by electromagnetic lenses, namely condenser, objective, and projector lenses. When a well-prepared specimen is placed in the electron beam, over the objective lens, the image of the tissue structure is projected on a fluorescent screen or a plate to photograph it. Of course, it is more complex than I just described, but that is a general overview of our work.

As I examined the cells through the electron microscope, I marveled at God's creative power. Looking at tissue samples magnified 10,000 times allowed me to see miraculous structures and marvelous arrangements. The cell is a complex unit of our body. There are billions of cells in our body, each one with a specific function. They all fit together like a perfectly timed watch, every one accomplishing its own work.

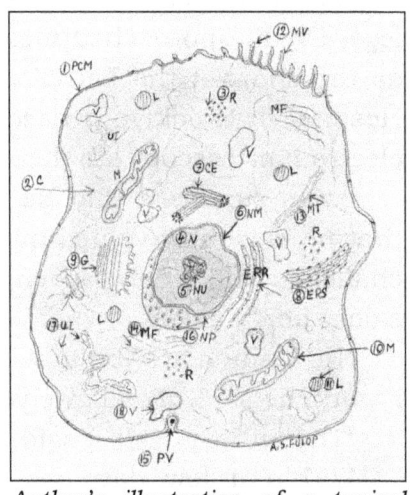

Author's illustration of a typical cell, showing the many, various components seen under the electron microscope.

Some people say this order is the result of a series of accidents, but I call it the miraculous creation of an intelligent person—the Creator of the universe. As I studied human, animal, and fish tissue, I could see the similarities. I could see how Darwin said that the similarities proved that we as humans had evolved from other creatures, but in light of being a creationist, I came to a different conclusion. The similarities prove that we came from the same divine hand of God. When I examined our cell structures and its accurate works and specific function for our good, I bowed my head before the mighty Creator who made all things and said, with the psalmist, "You formed my inward parts ... I will praise You, for I am fearfully and wonderfully made; Marvelous are Your works" (Ps. 139:13, 14). There wasn't a shadow of a doubt in my mind as to the supremacy of God and His authority in our lives.

After a successful few years at New York Medical College, Dr. Z. approached me. "Alex, I accepted a position as the chair of the Pathology Department at Methodist Hospital in Brooklyn. I need a qualified man to run the electron microscopy lab there. Would you come with me?"

I was surprised that he thought of me, and pleased that he obviously valued my work. I was up for another challenge and a new adventure. "How much would the salary be?" I asked.

"How much are you making now?" I told him my salary, and he said. "I will give you $1,000 more!"

"Then it is a deal!" I said.

Within a few days we moved from Manhattan to Brooklyn. I was excited about the opportunity to set up my laboratory from scratch. I was responsible for purchasing a microscope, a microtome to cut with, and all other instruments for the darkroom and lab. Within a few weeks we had all the tools necessary to begin our work. We conducted experiments and used electron microscopy to clarify diagnosis. A few doctors in the hospital used my lab for experiments, and they soon became my friends.

While working at the hospital, I also had a chance to meet the chaplain, who was a Methodist minister. We had nice talks together about the Bible and related subjects. He told me about the history of the Methodist Church and John Wesley. I had the privilege of telling him about the Seventh-day Adventist Church, and he respected me for my beliefs. We were good friends, and we prayed together many times.

In 1971 I had an experience I will never forget that involved sharing my faith with a fellow believer. Her name was Rebecca Abel. I met her on an unforgettable Sabbath morning, December 18, 1971, at the Jackson Heights Seventh-day Adventist Church in New York City.

Rebecca was a student at Andrews University in Berrien Springs, Michigan, but was visiting New York City on her way to Florida with her friend Vivika Black for the Christmas break. She was a history major with a full scholarship; she planned to be a teacher.

The two young women joined my Sabbath School class on that cold Sabbath morning. The lesson we discussed centered around the concept that giving is our greatest joy. After opening prayer we engaged in a wonderful discussion. We emphasized God's great gift, which is related so beautifully in John 3:16. We also discussed how we must respond to His love by giving what we have: our means, our talents, and ourselves.

Rebecca sat across from me. She seemed to be enjoying every part of the lesson, and she actively engaged in sharing her thoughts. Joy filled my heart as I led out, for here was a young visitor willing participating in the lesson. I felt the Spirit of God had been with us in that holy hour.

About eight hours later, I saw Rebecca again when we gathered at the church for ingathering. We had a small group of singers and musicians. The plan was to go door to door singing Christmas carols and ask for donations to help others during the holiday season.

As I approached the leader of the group, he said, "We have a new volunteer. Her name is Rebecca, and she is going to work with us tonight."

"We already know each other," I said. "She came to my Sabbath School this morning." I shook her hand and welcomed her again. Rebecca joined my daughter's group that night, and we set out. We had a marvelous experience that evening. The Lord blessed our effort, and we raised more than $1,000.

About nine o'clock we arrived back at the church. As soon as I entered the building, the head deacon came to me and said, "Alex, I received a telephone call from Jamaica Hospital. There was an accident with your daughter's group. One of the girls is injured. Please, go there and pick up the young people. They are waiting at the hospital."

I rushed to the hospital, and when I arrived I heard the sad story. At approximately 7:00 p.m. the group was crossing Liberty Avenue at 78th Street when an automobile struck Becky. Upon arriving at the hospital, they discovered she had broken several bones, was bruised from head to toe, and had suffered a number of internal injuries that was causing internal bleeding. She was in very critical condition.

Many prayers were offered on her behalf both at the scene of the accident and in the hospital by our youth and later by our pastor. In spite of the extent of her injuries, she never lost consciousness. We were able to talk to her, and she surrendered her life to Jesus. About midnight she went into surgery, but she never woke up from it. After many attempt to save her life, the surgeons finally pronounced her dead at 2:00 a.m. on Sunday morning.

Even though we hadn't known her for long, we were all in shock. However, many of us headed back out on Sunday evening to finish our ingathering campaign although our hearts were very heavy. We couldn't understand why the Lord had permitted the death of our dear sister. I suggested that we pray so we came together as a group and spread our sorrows before our God. We knew that we were not better than she was. We rededicated our lives to His service, to carry on the work. We asked the Lord to give us the victory to finish our church goal even as we were mourning. We gave thanks to God for the hope that at His glorious second coming we would meet our dear sister Rebecca. We all felt the Spirit of God resting on us in this united time of prayer.

The Lord comforted us with a great blessing that evening, helping us to collect another $1,500, which resulted in us reaching our final goal of raising $12,000.

So many thoughts ran through my head as we departed that Sunday evening from the church. *That was the last Sabbath School lesson that Rebecca participated in. What if I had failed to teach it well? Did I give my best? Were my words a comfort and hope to her in her last hours on this earth? Did I bring out the best from the Word of God?* As I mulled over these questions, I hoped beyond hope that God had used me.

I only saw Rebecca three times in my life, but she made an impact on me. First, I met her when she came to our church to worship her God, whom she loved so much. Second, I met her working for the Savior, in which she found much joy and happiness. And last, I saw her lying still at the funeral parlor. She came so suddenly and left that way too. But her memory remained with me for a long time. Her life reminds me of my Savior's words: "Who then is a faithful and wise servant, whom his master made ruler over his household, to give them food in due season? Blessed is that servant whom his master, when he comes, will find so doing" (Matt. 24:45, 46).

Someday sooner or later all of us will face death, unless our beloved Savior comes in our lifetime, which I am hoping for. The question is, where will our last day find us? Rebecca was working for God. She was visiting homes, distributing godly literature, and collecting money to help others when her life tragically ended. May we all work for the Lord every hour of every day, for we don't know when it might be our last.

After ten years of service, Dr. Z. came to me. "Alex, I have bad news," he said. "Because of a lack of money for research, I have to give up the electron microscopy lab!"

I was shocked! My mind immediately began questioning what was next. *Now what? What am I going to do? Where am I going to find a job?*

Dr. Z. saw the look of worry on my face, and he said, "Do not worry, Alex. I will not dismiss you until you find a job." It gave me a sense of security knowing that I wouldn't go without pay. "I have made arrangements with the Histology Department," he continued, "for you to work there half the day and spend the other half in the electron microscopy lab for the same salary until you will find a new job."

I thanked him for his generosity and kindness.

The histology lab was a distance from the hospital, but there was a shuttle that took me between the two labs. I worked at one in the morning and the other in the afternoon. Meanwhile, I looked for other work. One month passed and then two and still no work. I applied at a university and had an interview with them, but they turned me down. They did not tell me why I didn't get the job, but I suspected that it was because of my age. You see I was already fifty years old at the time. It appeared to me that they were looking for a younger individual. Elizabeth and I continued to pray and ask for God's guidance.

Than, after half a year of sending out resumes and interviewing for jobs, I was offered two positions at the same time. One position was at Loma Linda University in California and the one was close by at Brooklyn State University.

I decided that I would visit both locations and see which job was right for me. I first visited Brooklyn State University. They liked my background and experience in electron microscopy work. They were very nice to me and wanted to hire me right away. However, I told them that I had received another offer, and I wanted to check it out before making a final decision. As I left, I said, "If it is God's will, I will be back."

One of the doctors had a funny expression on his face when I made that statement, like "what kind of religious fanatic are we dealing with?" But both of the interviewing doctors were quiet.

I next flew out to Loma Linda. They paid for my airfare, which was a big blessing. They showed me the lab and explained my job responsibilities. They even loaned me a car to look around for real estate. I liked the work and the place, but I felt as if I was suffocating from the bad air. It was the middle of August, the worst time they said for humidity and smog. Because of the poor air quality, I turned down the position.

Upon arriving back in New York, I immediately headed back to Brooklyn State University to accept the job offer. They were very glad to see me. Then one of the female doctors, who became my superior for fifteen years, bent over and whispered in my ear, "It looks like it is the will of the Lord that you came back to us!"

I smiled at her and said, "Indeed!"

I enjoyed working with Dr. C., and we conducted a lot of research together. It was a team effort. She was the "head," and I was the "hands." We also taught electron microscopy to students working on their medical degree or doctorate. Dr. C. worked on the research, and I coordinated the technical part of preparing specimens for examination.

Because Dr. C. was Jewish, although she wasn't a practicing Jew, she never gave me any trouble over the Sabbath. Rather, she admired me for keeping it. I enjoyed many long discussions with her about religion. One day I told her that my faith was strengthened when I saw her. She asked me why.

"When I see a Jewish person," I said, "the Bible history comes to my mind. How God led the children of Israel into the Promised Land. And how tenderly and lovingly He cared for them, regardless of how many times they disappointed Him by their disobedience in the wilderness."

I continued, "I am a spiritual Israelite. God has a people on the earth, a chosen few, who have accepted Jesus as the promised Messiah. And we are going to the 'Promised Land' when He comes back for us a second time."

She listened, but it was too "unusual" of an idea for her to believe. As I experienced then and later on, the simple gospel message was often difficult for highly educated people to accept. I had seen the pattern before. It seemed that the more knowledge a person had, the less Bible belief they had in their heart.

I had another Jewish friend, a research scientist and professor at the university, who I walked with every second week to a local bank to cash our paychecks. We talked about many things on our thirty-five-minute walk. But our favorite subject was religion. One time I asked him, "There is one thing I do not understand; there are about 300 prophecies in the Old Testament about the coming Messiah. They describe the place, the manner, and the appearance of the Messiah, and the Jews still don't receive Him as the Messiah!"

He simply said, "He just doesn't fit the description!"

His response amazed me! How much more did God have to reveal?

After a fruitful and enjoyable fifteen years working at Brooklyn State University, I retired. They wanted me to stay longer, but I told them that my body was wearing out and needed to relax after the stresses of my life. They threw me a wonderful farewell party with many gifts and kind words.

Very shortly after retiring, Elizabeth and I moved to Chattanooga, Tennessee, to be closer to our family. We were so excited to no longer have work to worry about, but our retirement started off with a trial.

After settling in my wife complained that she didn't feel good. The doctor biopsied some tissue, and we waited for the test results. When the results were in, he scheduled an appointment with us and told us the bad news. "Ms. Fulop, I have bad news to tell you! You have cancer on your ovary."

We looked at each other, and right then and there we decided to place our faith in God and trust Him, no matter what the outcome. Whatever He permitted, we would take with dignity.

The doctor discussed our treatment options, and we scheduled surgery to remove the cancerous tissue. They removed the cancer and many of the glands nearby and then they began radiation therapy.

After a few treatments, she looked very strange. I felt that something was seriously wrong with her. I called our son-in-law, who is a physician, and he recommended that I call an ambulance. When the emergency medical technicians arrived, they took her to the hospital. The examination showed that the radiation almost killed her. After they stopped the procedure, she recovered. Now almost five years later she is doing quite well. We are very grateful for that.

As of today, she is eighty-two, and I am eighty-four. We praise our wonderful God for taking care of us, His children. After nineteen years of retirement, we are still active and enjoying life.

Conclusion

If there is one thing I have learned while living on this earth is that my story is His story! God has been with me every day of my life, protecting, leading, guiding, and saving me.

The Word of God says, "Remember His marvelous works which He has done, His wonders, and the judgments of His mouth, O seed of Israel His servant ... His chosen ones.... He is the Lord our God" (1 Chron. 16:12–14). So, I want to "remember His marvelous works" in my life. I want to remember what the Lord has done, and I encourage you to do the same.

He has blessed us so abundantly. We retired after forty years of work, and we have been married for fifty-nine years.

Jesus is our personal Savior, and we anxiously wait for His promised return. Jesus died for you, and He wants to take you to heaven. So cheer up, my friend! Trust in Him! Obey Him! You will be glad you did!

1954

2013

We invite you to view the complete
selection of titles we publish at:

www.TEACHServices.com

Scan with your mobiledevice
to go directly to our website.

Please write or email us your praises, reactions, or
thoughts about this or any other book we publish at:

P.O. Box 954
Ringgold, GA 30736
info@TEACHServices.com

TEACH Services, Inc., titles may be purchased in bulk for
educational, business, fund-raising, or sales promotional use.
For information, please e-mail:

BulkSales@TEACHServices.com

Finally, if you are interested in seeing
your own book in print, please contact us at

publishing@TEACHServices.com

We would be happy to review your manuscript for free.

www.ingramcontent.com/pod-product-compliance
Lightning Source LLC
Chambersburg PA
CBHW070544170426
43200CB00011B/2550